Paris

Travel Guide

Your Ultimate Insider's Handbook to Exploring Paris's Neighborhoods, Iconic Landmarks, Authentic Cuisine, Local Culture, Hidden Gems, and Must-See Attractions

Adrian Nakamura

Table of Contents

INTRODUCTION

Paris isn't simply a destination, it's a vibe, a cadence, a lens through which to use the world. For centuries, this place was a nucleus of global culture, from which the world was collectively given its sense of art, style, food, literature, and philosophy. It's a country that clings to tradition but has always sought ways to remake itself. Approach it with an open mind and a sense of curiosity, and Paris will reward you with memories.

The intention of this guide is to help you visit Paris slowly, mindfully. Not merely to tick off landmarks but to feel what gives the city life and perhaps what's needed most now. Stroll along grand boulevards now, where the architecture retains some of the grandeur of past centuries. Check out the morning market stalls — cheerily filled with flowers, crusty baguettes, and cheeses that locals still take the time to debate about and taste. Sit at a café and observe how everyone is taking their time. Time stops here — well, not stops, but it slows down, like a good coffee and/or a glass of good wine on the table.

Of course, the museums are world-famous. But even more than the art, it's the way light hits a wall or how people freeze midstep in front of a painting that leaves an impression. Stand silently before the Mona Lisa at the Louvre, or watch the Impressionists shimmer at the Musée d'Orsay. These are the moments that you never forget. You don't have to be an expert — just show up with your attention and attention span.

Boat along the Seine or ascend the Eiffel Tower for a panorama that can extend to the city's edge. Stroll the winding lanes of the Marais, enjoy a glass of wine in the Latin Quarter, or take a seat on a park bench near the Luxembourg Gardens and simply watch the world go by. Getting lost, even in Paris, is just part of the experience. And when darkness falls, the mood shifts yet again. The cafés sparkle, the monuments shine, and the city vibrates gently with music, talk, and footsteps on cobblestone streets. Dinner can stretch to two hours or longer — not that it needs to, but that it can.

Paris has its quirks. It is, at some points, frustrating, confusing, or mildly distant. But it rewards patience. If you take your time and allow yourself to observe the details— the flicker of a candle in a bistro, the smell of a baking loaf from a corner bakery, the rooftops tinted in gold at sundown—you will begin to feel the pulse. First things, this is not a guidebook that tells you how to do Paris. It's simply in it to help you appreciate more of it. I've divided it by neighborhood and experience and added practical tips, walks to take, favorite places to eat and sleep, and how to connect with the local culture. Take what may work, leave what doesn't, and make it yours.

Welcome to Paris. Take your time. Look around. Stay curious.

Central Paris, home to some 2.3 million people, sits between a ring road and the Seine, which runs east to west through the heart of the city. The Right Bank (Rive Droite) is to the north of the river, while the Left Bank (Rive Gauche) is to the south. The Notre Dame cathedral is on a little island in the Seine, dead center of the city.

Paris is organized into 20 administrative districts called arrondissements that spiral out from the center. Paris zip codes are a reminder of this: for instance, 75007 means it's in the 7th arrondissement. The Metro covers all districts and is the primary means by which locals travel. (The Eiffel Tower, for reference, is on the Left Bank in the 7th arrondissement, close to the Trocadéro Metro stop.)

Every neighborhood (arrondissement) in Paris has landmarks and a vibe. Here's a quick look:

Heart of Old Paris: Around the Île de la Cité, this area is home to the city's oldest buildings, places of worship, and central views along the river.

Champs-Élysées: One of the city's most well-known avenues, filled with monuments, shops, and views from the Place de la Concorde to the Arc de Triomphe.

Major Museums Area: Just to the west of the center, this district includes Paris's most lauded art museums and some stylish gardens.

Opéra Neighborhood: An affluent district of grand buildings, shopping, and cultural landmarks, centered around the Opéra Garnier.

Eiffel Tower District: Home to the Eiffel Tower, this neighborhood also includes bustling markets, museums, and a quaint street.

Top Paris Moments

Eiffel Tower – The city's most famous symbol. Go up for the view or admire it from below.

Open daily: 9 a.m.–midnight in summer; 9:30 a.m.–11:45 p.m. the rest of the year.

The Louvre – Massive museum with the Mona Lisa, Venus de Milo, and much more.

Wednesday–Mon, 9 a.m.–6 p.m.; closed Tuesday.

Sainte-Chapelle – Tiny Gothic chapel with breathtaking stained glass.

Open daily 9 a.m.–7 p.m.; closes at 5 p.m. in winter.

Versailles – Extravagant royal palace with gardens, fountains, and Marie-Antoinette's retreat.

Closed Mondays; various hours for palace, gardens, and Trianon.

Champs-Élysées – An Iconic avenue for walking, shopping, or people-watching.
Runs from Place de la Concorde to the Arc de Triomphe.

Montmartre & Sacré-Cœur – Hilltop neighborhood with art, views, and the white basilica.

The church opens daily from 6:30 a.m. to 10:30 p.m.; the dome climb is open during the day.

Orsay Museum – Housed in a former train station, it's full of Impressionist art.

Tue–Sun; open late Wed; closed Mon.

Pompidou Centre – Modern art and funky architecture with a great rooftop.
Open Wed–Mon, 11 a.m.–9 p.m.; closed Tues.

Luxembourg Gardens – Locals' favorite park with statues, lawns, and toy sailboats.
Always open, great for a relaxed afternoon.

Galeries Lafayette Rooftop – Free terrace with killer views of the Eiffel Tower and skyline.
Open during store hours; check for sunset.

Canal Saint-Martin – Trendy area with calm water, iron bridges, and hip cafés.
No ticket is needed—just walk and soak it in.

Rue Cler – A small market street packed with local food shops and cafés.
Most shops are open Tue–Saturday; closed Sun afternoons and all day Mon.

Notre-Dame Cathedral – Still closed for repairs, but you can admire it from the outside.

Rodin Museum – Sculptures in a peaceful garden setting.
Tue–Sun, 10 a.m.–6:30 p.m.; closed Mon.

Cluny Museum – Medieval art, including the famous unicorn tapestries.
Tue–Sun; closed Mon; some nights open late.

Orangerie Museum – Home to Monet's huge Water Lilies panels.
Wed–Mon, 9 a.m.–6 p.m.; closed Tues.

Army Museum & Napoleon's Tomb – Grand tomb and a big military collection.
Open daily 10 a.m.–6 p.m.; tomb open till 9 p.m. on Tuesdays.

Opéra Garnier – Stunning old opera house with a Chagall ceiling.
Usually open daily from 10 a.m.–4 p.m.; until 5 p.m. in summer.

Jacquemart-André Museum – A 19th-century mansion filled with art.
Open daily 10 a.m.–6 p.m.; late Mon for special exhibits.

Père Lachaise Cemetery – Peaceful cemetery where many famous figures are buried.
Open daily; hours vary by day and season.

Picasso Museum – Rotating exhibits in a grand townhouse.
Tue–Fri 10:30 a.m.–6 p.m.; Sat–Sun from 9 a.m.; closed Mon.

Arc de Triomphe – Climb for great views down the Champs-Élysées.
Open daily 10 a.m.–11 p.m.; shorter hours in winter.

Carnavalet Museum – Free museum dedicated to the history of Paris.
Tue–Sun, 10 a.m.–6 p.m.; closed Mon.

Marmottan Museum – Focuses on Monet and his circle.

Tue–Sun, 10 a.m.–6 p.m.; Thu open late; closed Mon.

Panthéon – Final resting place for many of France's greats.

Open daily 10 a.m.–6:30 p.m.; closes at 6 p.m. Oct–Mar.

Your Paris Game Plan

The sample itineraries below show how much you can fit into a well-planned day in Paris—especially if you start early, wear comfortable shoes, and don't mind a little caffeine boost. That said, avoid cramming too much into your schedule. Paris rewards slow moments—an unplanned stop at a bakery, a surprise discovery down a quiet street. Leave space for the unexpected, and you'll enjoy the city even more. A week is ideal for a good Paris experience, but if you're staying for fewer days, these suggestions will help you pick what matters most.

Day 1: History and First Impressions

Start your trip by diving into Paris's oldest areas. Begin with a walking route that covers Notre-Dame Cathedral (you can't go inside right now, but it's still worth seeing), then stroll through the Latin Quarter's winding streets. Visit Sainte-Chapelle for its jaw-dropping stained glass, one of the city's hidden masterpieces. Stop and relax in Luxembourg Garden—locals love it for its calm atmosphere and tree-shaded chairs. Afterward, explore the Cluny Museum to see medieval art and relics. Then, cross town to the Opéra Garnier—one of Paris's most impressive buildings. End the day with a sunset cruise on the Seine; watching the city light up from the water is a great way to wrap up your first day.

Day 2: Art, Avenues, and Evenings

Start the morning at the Louvre—go early to beat the lines and focus on a few key sections (the museum is huge, so don't try to see it all). Then walk up the Champs-Élysées, passing the Arc de Triomphe and heading down to the Tuileries Garden. This classic Paris walk blends grandeur and calm. You can stop at the Orangerie Museum at the far end of the garden to see Monet's Water Lilies and more. In the evening, head to Île Saint-Louis for a quiet dinner at a local bistro. Afterward, take a slow walk along the Seine, especially near Notre-Dame—it's beautifully lit at night.

Day 3: Impressionism and Reflection

Spend the morning visiting the Orsay Museum, housed in a former train station and packed with Impressionist and post-Impressionist masterpieces. After that, continue to the Rodin Museum nearby, where the sculptures are displayed both indoors and in a peaceful garden. After lunch, visit the Army Museum and Napoleon's Tomb, located inside Les Invalides. From there, take a break in the Rue Cler area: browse the food shops, sit down at a café, and enjoy the neighborhood feel. Later, walk along the Left Bank near the river, and end your day with a scenic night tour by open-top bus, vintage car, or even a sidecar motorcycle if you want something different.

Day 4: Versailles Day Trip

Catch the RER C train to Versailles in the morning—it takes about 45 minutes. Start with the main château and Hall of Mirrors, then explore the formal gardens and fountains. If time allows, visit the Trianon Palaces and the Queen's Hamlet. Versailles has a few on-site restaurants and cafés, or you can pack a picnic. After a full day, return to Paris in the early evening and have dinner near your hotel or in a nearby neighborhood.

Day 5: The Marais District

Spend today in the historic and trendy Marais. Begin at the Carnavalet Museum, which focuses on Parisian history. Have lunch at Place des Vosges (one of Paris's oldest and most beautiful squares) or along Rue des Rosiers, known for its lively Jewish eateries. In the afternoon, choose one or two sights nearby—the Pompidou Centre, the Jewish Museum, the Picasso Museum, or Père Lachaise Cemetery are all in or near the area. Don't try to do all of them in one go. End the evening with a visit to the Eiffel Tower—go around sunset if possible. You can admire it from the Trocadéro Plaza or head up to the top for sweeping views.

Day 6: A Bit Outside or a Bit of Shopping

If you're up for a day trip, take the train to Giverny to visit Monet's home and garden (especially beautiful in spring/summer) or to Chartres for its magnificent Gothic cathedral. If you'd rather stay local, dedicate today to shopping. Start in the Marais or Saint-Germain for boutique finds, or explore the grands magasins (big department stores) like Galeries Lafayette and Printemps. Stroll the Champs-Élysées and stop at cafés or patisseries as needed. Climb the Arc de Triomphe in the evening for one of the best night views of the city.

Day 7: Last Stops and Slow Moments

Take Bus 69 for a budget-friendly sightseeing route—it passes several major landmarks. Revisit a favorite spot or check out places you missed: Montmartre, Sacré-Cœur, Père Lachaise, or quieter museums like the Jacquemart-André or Marmottan. If the weather is good, sit outside at a café and soak in your final hours. If it's raining, enjoy a long lunch and browse a bookstore or art gallery. Leave time to pick up any last-minute gifts or treats to take home.

Getting Started

The steps in advance to make your Paris visit stress free Mind these basics and you will avoid a last-minute problem and be free to enjoy your time."

Make Sure Your Passport and Travel Documents Are In Order

Make sure your passport won't expire within six months from your return date — and if it does, renew it before you go. Regular filing may take as long as six weeks, potentially longer. As well, verify any entry requirements currently in place, like those related to COVID-19. Some countries might still require proof of vaccination or a recent negative test.

Plan Your Transportation: If you're flying internationally, book your flight early to get the best rates and the least amount of connection time. When in Paris, decide how you want to get around: metro, bus, walk, or even bike rentals. If you will be going to places outside the city (like Versailles or Giverny), figure out train tickets, rail passes, or rental cars beforehand.

Reserve Accommodations Early: Hotels and rentals can sell out during the high season or surrounding large events. The sooner you book, the better choice and price you will have. Think about the neighborhood that fits your travel style — central and walkable or quiet and more local.

Pre-Book Top Attractions: Timed reservations are often required at popular sites like the Louvre, Sainte-Chapelle, Orangerie, and Versailles. You may also want to book in advance for the Eiffel Tower, the Catacombs, and the Conciergerie, particularly during peak months. Many of those places have limited or no walk-up tickets.

Get a Paris Museum Pass: If you're going to check off several major museums and monuments, this pass can save you money and wait time. You can buy it online and use it to book timed entries to most participating attractions.

Look Into Travel Insurance: Consider whether trip insurance is worthwhile for your plans. It can assist with cancellations, lost bags, or medical problems. Check if your existing health or homeowners/renters insurance already includes some travel coverage.

Notify Your Bank: Tell your bank you'll be using your card overseas to prevent getting blocked for suspicious activity. Find out whether foreign transaction fees apply. For Europe, you will want a debit or credit card that is both contactless and requires a PIN. Euros can be withdrawn from ATMs when you arrive (**1€=1,09$**), so there's no need to bring large amounts of cash.

Get Your Phone Ready: If staying connected on the go is a priority, sign up for an international plan with your carrier. Or use Wi-Fi, widely available in Paris. Download useful apps ahead of your trip — Google Maps, a French-English translator, maps of the Paris Metro, and restaurant finders are all useful.

Pack Light: You'll likely be schlepping your bag more than you think upstairs, down cobbled streets, or onto a metro platform. Travel with only one carry-on suitcase and a small day pack if possible. The "Practicalities" chapter includes a complete packing checklist for reference.

Be Aware and Street Smart: Pickpockets are real, especially at crowded tourist spots and on the Metro. Stay awake in situations that aren't uncomfortable, like loud, heated debates or people running into you. A money belt or neck pouch for your passport, cards, and cash. Take only what you need for the day in a front pocket or zipped bag.

Stay Cool in the Heat: Ask me how I know (it can get hot, especially in July and August). Stay at a hotel with air conditioning, and try to schedule most of your walking or sightseeing early in the morning and late in the afternoon. Rest indoors or in shade parks in midday.

Allow Yourself to Be Flexible: Don't overplan every hour. Leave time for the spontaneous — an outdoor lunch, browsing a bookstore, watching street performers, or simply sitting at a café. With a slower pace, you can absorb the atmosphere and savor the little things.

Enjoy Like a Local: Bring a picnic and sit by the Seine, indulge in a long meal at a cozy bistro, or join a friendly game of boules in the park. These simple pleasures are some of the reasons why I fell in love with this city, and I hope you will as well.

Best Time to Visit

Paris is lovely any time of year, but that beauty can be very different depending on when you visit. Whether October 2023 is your best time to visit, the weather, crowds, cost, or special events matter most to you.

Spring (March to May)

Spring is the best time to visit. The weather begins to warm up, flowers bloom in parks and gardens, and the city feels fresh and alive after winter. Temperatures are in the low 50s to high 60s°F (10–20°C). Expect longer days and occasional rain, so bring a light coat and an umbrella. This is also when tourists begin to come back, again particularly in May, so secure accommodations in advance.

Summer (June to August)

Summer means long, golden days and bustling streets. Outdoor cafes, river cruises, and parks are glorious. And temperatures when the sun's out can reach the upper 80s°F (30°C+), and not all buildings have air conditioning, so try to pick your lodging carefully. July and August are high season for travel — lines are long, and prices rise. Given that many locals are out of town in August, while the tourist sites keep on operating, some small shops, cafés, and restaurants will take August off.

Fall (September to November)

Fall is another excellent time to visit. Temperatures remain pleasant through September and early October. The city quiets just a little as summer crowds depart and fall color appears in parks such as the Tuileries and Luxembourg Gardens. The cultural life resumes — concerts, exhibits, festivals are in full swing. Bring layers; temperatures gradually cool, and evenings can be cold.

Winter (December to February)

In the winter months, Paris is cold but enchantingly beautiful. Temperatures typically remain above freezing but can be wet, with occasional snow or rain. Tourist numbers shrink, an ideal time for museum-going and strolling. Cafés are particularly cozy, and prices for flights and hotels are generally more affordable. December is decked out with holiday lights and Christmas markets, and January and February tend to be quieter but no less appealing. Just dress for the elements — warm coats, scarves, gloves, and waterproof shoes are a must.

Summary

- **Visit in April** to early June or September to early October for mild weather and blooming parks

- If you want a **crowd-free experience** and still a festive mood, go here in winter, especially in December and February.

- If **summer** energy is your thing and you can handle heat and crowds, go for late June or early July.

- **To pay less**, try January, February, or late November, when prices and crowds are at a low.

- **No matter the season**, there's something special about Paris — you simply need to figure out what kind of trip you want..

Packing Tips

Packing the right way can ensure a smoother trip. There's plenty of walking, unpredictable weather, and random staircases without elevators — shoot for light, launch, and practical.

Clothing

- **Bring walking shoes** you can stand on. Many streets are cobblestone, and you'll be doing a lot of walking. Don't bring heels along unless you intend to wear them.

- **Dress in layers**. The weather can change rapidly — chilly mornings, warm afternoons. Even in summer, bring a light sweater or jacket.

- **Do not dress like a tourist**. Parisians dress neatly. Good jeans if clean and fitted. Neutral colors and uncomplicated outfits are good.

- **For winter**: A warm coat, scarf, gloves, hat, and waterproof shoes. It gets cold, wet, and windy.

- **In the summer**: Wear lightweight, breathable fabrics. Pack sunglasses, sunscreen, and perhaps a small fan or cooling towel if you're heat-sensitive.

Essentials

- **Travel documents**: Passport, ID, tickets, insurance, and printed confirmations.

- **Daypack or small crossbody bag**: For day-to-day. Stow it and keep it close to you and zipped, you know, on public transit.

- **Money belt or hidden pouch**: (Use in crowded areas for passports and backup cash/cards).

- **Phone charger and plug adapter**: France uses the European standard (Type C/E plugs, 230V).

- **Reusable water bottle**: You can drink from the tap in Paris.

- **Compact umbrella**: Rainstorms can appear out of nowhere, particularly in spring and fall.

Toiletries & Medications

- **Bring only what you need**. There are pharmacies on every corner in Paris.

- **Bring your daily medications** in original pham packaging, with copies of prescriptions when needed.

- **Have a small first aid kit** with band-aids, painkillers, and general supplies.

Extras That Help

- **Guidebook** or this one, download some notes

- **Apps**: Google Maps (for offline maps), metro, translator, and restaurant reviews.

- **Foldable tote bag**: Perfect for groceries or additional shopping.

- **Backups** of essential documents, whether stored separately or digitally in your email or cloud storage.

Luggage Advice

- Attempt to travel with just a single carry-on and a small personal item or backpack. You'll also save time, avoiding lost luggage and moving more easily through Metro stations, hotel stairs, and sidewalks.

- If you are checking a bag, put a change of clothes and the essentials in your carry-on just in case.

As well as less time worrying about stuff and more time enjoying Paris

Pro-Tips

Before you hop on your flight, take a little time to prep. These tips will help your trip go more smoothly, avoid hassles, and save time once you're there.

Health & Safety Updates

Check for any current health guidelines, safety alerts, or travel restrictions before you leave. Visit the U.S. State Department's travel site (www.travel.state.gov) for destination-specific info and the CDC's travel section (www.cdc.gov/travel) for health-related updates like vaccinations or disease advisories.

Tourist Information Centers

Paris has official tourist offices (referred to as "TI" in this guide), which offer maps, brochures, museum passes, and tickets to attractions, concerts, and events. Lines can be long, and there may be a small extra fee, so use them mainly for information and not last-minute ticket purchases.

- **Main TI**: Hôtel de Ville (29 Rue de Rivoli, open daily 10 a.m.–6 p.m.)
- **Airport TIs**: Located in both major airports, open early and close late for arriving travelers.

More info: www.parisinfo.com

Language Basics

While many Parisians speak some English, it's polite to use basic French phrases. Start each interaction with "Bonjour, Madame/Monsieur" and end with "Au revoir." A few handy words:

- *Bonjour* = Hello / Good day
- *Pardon* = Excuse me
- *S'il vous plaît* = Please
- *Merci* = Thank you .
- *Au revoir* = Goodbye

Even a small effort goes a long way and tends to get better service.

Time Zone

France is 6 hours ahead of Eastern Time and 9 hours ahead of Pacific Time. Use your phone's world clock to keep track of the time difference and avoid jet lag mishaps—especially when planning your arrival or calling home.

Business Hours

Most smaller shops open from **10 a.m. to 12 p.m.**, then take a break and reopen from **2 p.m. to 7 p.m.**, Monday through Saturday. Many close all day Sunday.

Larger stores, grocery shops, and malls near tourist areas (like Galeries Lafayette, Carrousel du Louvre, Champs-Élysées, and the Marais) often stay open daily.

Street markets and bakeries usually shut by **noon on Sunday**.

Electrical Outlets

France uses **220 volts** and **two round-pin plugs (Type C or E)**. Most modern electronics (phones, laptops, tablets, cameras, etc.) work automatically with the voltage, but you'll still need a plug adapter. You can find these at most travel stores or airports before your trip.

Around Town

Bookstores with English Books

- *Shakespeare and Company* (37 Rue de la Bûcherie, 75005): Open daily, 10 a.m. to 10 p.m. — a must-visit.
- *Smith&Son* (248 Rue de Rivoli, near Tuileries): Mon–Sat, 9 a.m.–7 p.m.; Sun, 12 p.m.–7 p.m.
- *Abbey Bookshop* (29 Rue de la Parcheminerie, Latin Quarter): Closed Sundays.
- *San Francisco Book Company* (17 Rue Monsieur le Prince, near Luxembourg Gardens): Open Thurs–Tues from 10 a.m.–12 p.m. (closed Wednesday).

Laundry Services

Ask your hotel front desk or concierge to direct you to the nearest self-service laundry (*laverie*) or full-service cleaner.

Public Restrooms

Most museums have restrooms available even if you're not visiting the exhibits—just ask. There are also **public toilets** throughout the city. Some are free and automated; others have attendants (it's customary to leave a small tip in that case).

Tobacco Shops (Tabacs)

Marked with a red "Tabac" sign, these small stores are everywhere. Besides cigarettes, they often sell **Metro tickets**, **postage stamps**, and sometimes **bus passes**. Handy to know when you need small items in a pinch.

EXCLUSIVE BONUSES FOR READERS

Thank you for choosing *Paris Travel Guide*! To help you make the most of your trip, I've put together three valuable bonus resources designed to make your Paris adventure smoother, more enjoyable, and unforgettable. Here's what you'll get:

✓ **Paris Neighborhood Cheat Sheets** – Handy, printable guides that break down each key district with top sights, dining spots, transport tips, and hidden gems—perfect for exploring like a local.

✓ **Essential French for Travelers Quick Guide** – A compact, easy-to-use phrasebook with must-know French expressions and pronunciation tips to help you navigate daily interactions with confidence.

✓ **7-Day Paris Itinerary** – A thoughtfully crafted day-by-day plan covering iconic landmarks and charming neighborhoods, balanced with time for discovery and relaxation.

To unlock your bonuses, simply scan the QR code below with your phone and gain instant access.

These exclusive tools are available only to readers of this guide—you won't find them anywhere else. Dive in now and elevate your Paris experience to the fullest!

WELCOME TO PARIS

Charles de Gaulle Airport (CDG)

The biggest international airport in Paris, **CDG**, has three terminals: **T1, T2,** and **T3**. The majority of flights from the **U.S.** arrive in **Terminals 1** or **2**. The free, frequently running **CDGVAL** light-rail connects all terminals, though if you are transferring between terminals, allow yourself up to an hour. Inside it are Paris tourism service counters, free **Wi-Fi, ATMs, cafés, shops**, and VAT refund desks (in the check-in zones).

Getting from CDG to the City

- **Taxi or Uber**: Taxis charge a flat fare: €55 to the Right Bank and €60 to the Left Bank (baggage is included for up to four passengers). Dec 1, 2021, 05:30 AM: Keep reading for advice. When returning to the airport from the city, the best option is to have your hotel call a taxi for you.

Uber is an option, but less convenient: pickup points are not always clearly designated, and Ubers aren't allowed to use bus lanes, making the ride often slower than by taxi.

- **RoissyBu**s: This airport bus travels between CDG and the Opéra metro station in central Paris. It operates every 15–30 minutes from 06:00 to 23:00.

  o Fare: €15

  o **Drive time**: ~1 hour, traffic permitting

  o You can buy **tickets at airport** kiosks or on the bus.

  o **At the Opéra**, you'll find a convenient transfer to the metro, or you can hop into a cab for a quick ride to your hotel.

- **RER B Suburban Train**: The quickest and cheapest way to get to central Paris.

  o Fare: €11.50

  o How often: Once every 10–15 minutes during 5:00 a.m.– 12:00 a.m.

  o Travel time: 35–45 minutes approximately

The RER B also stops at Gare du Nord, Châtelet-Les Halles, Saint-Michel, and Luxembourg, all of which are well connected to the metro.

Roissy CDG has 2 RER stations: one in Terminal 2, the second at Roissypole close to Terminal 3. From Terminals 1 or 2, catch the CDGVAL shuttle to the RER station if necessary. Just follow the signs for "Train" or "RER."

Some Important Details

You may be told that Parisians are aloof or unwilling to speak English. That's a myth. Although people here can seem more reserved or formal, most are polite, and many, especially those in tourist towns, know English. Do not expect cheery small talk or big smiles. In France, service is of the professional, not chatty, kind. Waiters aren't being impolite — they're focused on their job of getting things done.

Cultural tip: Don't rush. Parisians relish the slow pace the enjoy the moment, whether that's taking a leisurely walk, enjoying a meal, or sipping coffee at a sidewalk café. If you are patient, polite, and demonstrate even a modicum of respect for local customs, your interaction will usually be warm and respectful..

Other Arrival Points

Orly Airport (ORY)

Located south of the city, Orly is smaller but well-organized and often used for European or domestic flights. The airport has **tourist information desks** inside arrivals where you can buy **Museum Passes** and **public transport tickets**.

- **Taxi fares**: €32 to the Left Bank, €37 to the Right Bank
- **OrlyBus**: Connects to RER B for fast access to stops like **Luxembourg, Châtelet, Notre-Dame**, and **Gare du Nord**
- **Uber** is available, with similar pros and cons as at CDG.

Train Stations in Paris

Paris has **six main train stations**, each serving different parts of France and Europe.

- **Gare du Nord**: For Eurostar from London and trains to northern France and Belgium
- **Gare de Lyon**: Southern and eastern France, including Lyon, Marseille, and the Alps
- **Gare Montparnasse**: Western France, including Brittany and Bordeaux
- **Gare Saint-Lazare**: Normandy and northwest France
- **Gare de l'Est**: Eastern France and Germany
- **Gare d'Austerlitz**: Central France and night trains

For schedules and bookings:

- **Domestic trains**: sncf.com
- **European rail**: bahn.com
- **TGV & high-speed trains**: Pre-book online (InOui)

- Consider checking if a **rail pass** is worth it, depending on how many trips you plan outside Paris.

How to Get Around

Paris is a highly walkable city, known for its compact layout and excellent public transportation. The Metro is among the most efficient in Europe, and you're almost always within a 10-minute walk of a station. Buses also cover the city extensively, offering another easy way to get around. To get your bearings quickly, refer to the fold-out Metro map at the back of this book and visit the official public transport website for schedules and updates: https://www.ratp.fr/.

Buy a **Navigo Easy card** early in your trip—it makes everything simpler—and learn a few key Metro and bus lines to get around confidently.

Buying Tickets

Paris uses a single ticketing system for the Metro, public buses, trams, and RER suburban trains within the city. The **Navigo Easy card** (rechargeable, €2) is your best bet. Load it with:

- **Single rides** (€1.90 each)
- **10-ride pass** (€14.90 for Zones 1–2)
- **1-day pass (Navigo Jour)** (€7.50 for central Paris, Zones 1–2)
- **1-day pass with extra zones** (€12.40, includes places like Versailles in Zone 4)

You can buy or reload your Navigo Easy at any staffed Metro station, vending machine, or even some **tobacco** shops. You can also set up a digital version in the **RATP app** and tap your phone to enter the Metro or board buses.

Using the Metro

The Paris Metro runs daily from **5:30 a.m. to 12:30 a.m.**, with extended hours on **Friday and Saturday nights**. Trains are frequent and well-marked.

Each line is color-coded and numbered, with stops listed by direction (e.g., *Direction: La Défense*). At the gate, hold your Navigo card or phone over the purple scanner. Wait for the green light and the "ding" sound before walking through.

Inside the system, be ready for long walks—some stations involve multiple staircases and corridors. To transfer lines, follow signs marked **Correspondance** (transfer). When exiting, look for **Sortie** signs (exit), and use posted area maps to choose the best exit.

Metro Tips

- Metro maps are available inside this book, at all stations, and online.

- Free paper maps can also be picked up at hotels or tourist offices.

- Watch for pickpockets, especially around ticket machines, turnstiles, and crowded platforms. Keep bags zipped and valuables secure.

Using the RER (Suburban Train)

The **RER** is similar to the Metro but faster and designed for longer distances. It connects central Paris with suburbs and major sights like **Versailles** or **CDG Airport**.

Lines are marked A through E and shown as **thicker lines** on maps. Fares depend on the destination—travel outside Paris costs more than standard Metro rides. Some RER trains skip stops, so check the platform signs or screen displays before boarding to be sure your station is listed.

Using City Buses

Buses in Paris are a great way to see the city above ground, especially if you're not in a rush. They're clean, reliable, and serve many routes that connect areas not always linked by Metro.

Most bus stops have clear signs with **route maps**, **live arrival info**, and **neighborhood maps**. Some even include **USB charging ports** for phones. Buses use the same ticketing system as the Metro and RER, so your **Navigo Easy card** works here too—just make sure it's loaded before you board.

You **must validate your card** when entering. Tap your Navigo card on the reader near the driver. If you're using a paper ticket (not recommended), insert it into the machine next to the entrance.

Transfers and Limitations

Your Navigo Easy card allows you to transfer between **bus lines or between a bus and a tram** within **90 minutes** of your first ride. But keep in mind:

- You **can't** transfer from a **bus to the Metro or RER** on the same ride.

- You **can't** use one fare for multiple rides on the **same bus line** in that time frame.

If you're planning several stops or line changes, a **day pass (Navigo Jour)** may be more cost-effective.

Tips for Bus Travel

- Enter through the front door and exit through the middle or rear.

- During busy times, buses can be slower than the Metro due to traffic.

- Routes like **Bus 69** or **Bus 42** double as budget-friendly sightseeing tours—they pass by many major landmarks.

- Most bus stops display real-time arrival info, so you'll know how long you'll wait.

To ride the bus, tap your **Navigo card** on the purple pad by the front door. Inside the bus, screens display upcoming stops. When your stop is near, press the red **"stop" button** to signal the driver. Use the **middle or back doors** to exit.

Avoid rush hours—**weekdays from 8:00 to 9:30 a.m. and 5:30 to 7:30 p.m.**—when buses get crowded and the Metro is usually faster.

Some especially scenic and useful bus lines:

- **Bus 69**: Runs from **Rue Cler** to **Père Lachaise Cemetery**, passing landmarks like the **Musée**

 d'Orsay, **Île Saint-Louis**, and **Le Marais**.

- **Bus 73**: It offers a ride up the **Champs-Élysées** from the **Orsay Museum** to the **Arc de**

  Triomphe—great views along the way.

Ask your hotel receptionist which nearby lines work best for your sightseeing plans.

By Uber

Uber works reliably in Paris and generally offers a smoother experience than regular taxis. Drivers tend to be friendlier and more flexible, and prices are usually similar to cab fares. You can request a ride through the app or even by text if needed.

That said, there are some downsides:

- Uber vehicles **can't use bus lanes**, which makes them slower in heavy traffic.

- During **rush hours or airport runs**, taxis are often faster and cheaper, with **flat rates** and **set pick-up points**.

- Uber pricing is **dynamic**—fares rise during peak times, and you need to set a meeting spot in advance since pickups aren't allowed just anywhere.

By Taxi

Taxis in Paris are a good choice for short trips, especially if you're not traveling solo. Fares are fixed and regulated.

- Base fare: **€2.60**

- Minimum charge: **€7.30**

- A typical 20-minute ride (e.g., Bastille to Eiffel Tower): around **€25**

- Surcharges apply for rush hours, nights, Sundays, extra passengers, and luggage

Each taxi holds up to four people, though some drivers may prefer fewer. Larger groups should **pre-book a van-style taxi**.

To hail a cab, wave from the curb or go to a taxi stand (look for the **circled "T" symbol** on maps). You can also call in English:

- **G7 Taxis**: +33 1 41 27 66 99

- Same-day bookings cost €4; advance bookings are €7

Tipping is simple: just round up to the nearest euro or add about **€0.50 to €1**, especially if the driver helps with bags.

Tip: Cabs can be hard to find when it's raining, late at night, or after the Metro closes. For early airport or train departures, have your hotel arrange a taxi the day before.

By Bike

Paris is a bike-friendly city, mostly flat and full of dedicated bike lanes (over **370 miles of them**). Cyclists can often use lanes shared with taxis and buses, but stay alert—traffic can be quick and unpredictable.

For bike paths in your area, check **paris.fr** or pick up a **"Paris à Vélo"** map at Tourist Info centers, newsstands, or bookstores.

Bike rentals and tours:

- **Bike About Tours**: Near Hôtel de Ville; rental ~€20/day, €17 half-day

- **Fat Tire Tours**: Near the Eiffel Tower (24 Rue Edgar Faure, Métro Dupleix or La Motte-Picquet–Grenelle); ~€4/hour

- Both also offer excellent guided biking tours.

Vélib' is Paris's public bike-sharing system (vélo + libre = "bike freedom") with thousands of stations around the city. Ideal for short, one-way rides. Use the **app or credit card** to rent.

Lime also operates **e-bikes and scooters**, which you can unlock and pay for using the **Lime app** (www.lime).

Money

France uses the euro (€); at this writing, the exchange rate is **about €1=$1.10**. An easy way to approximate the price in dollars is to add approximately 10% to any euro sum. So, for instance, €10 translates to about $11, and €50 is roughly $55. For live rates, visit sites such as oanda.com.

For spending in Paris, using a credit card is the easiest and safest choice for most purchases — from big-ticket items such as hotel stays or museum tickets to smaller transactions at bakeries, markets, or cafés. Most establishments now accept contactless payments, so make sure your card includes this feature (look for the symbol with four curved lines). Always memorise your four-digit PINs for all debit and credit cards in the event you are asked to enter it — particularly at unmanned machines or smaller vendors.

For cash, withdraw euros from an ATM (distributeur) with your debit card. You won't need to carry a lot of currency: You can find ATMs everywhere, and they usually offer better exchange rates than kiosks at the airport or currency booths. But carrying a little cash is helpful for tipping, paying at smaller shops, or for card machine failures.

Always try to pay at the register rather than via self-service machines — Metro ticket kiosks, for instance — and if you can pay with a card, bring a chip-and-PIN card, since for whatever reason, sometimes those things won't accept foreign cards. When that happens, try to find an attended window or pay cash. If you're not sure, ask a staff member for help.

That way, it keeps your cards and cash safely stored away. A money belt or neck pouch that you wear under your clothes is a good way to protect your valuables, especially in crowded places such as train stations or tourist areas.

About Tipping

In France, tipping is much less formal than in the United States. It usually comes with the bill, but small gestures of appreciation are always welcome.

In restaurants and cafés, a service charge (service compris) of around 12–15% is generally included in the menu prices. There's no need to tip on top of that, but if your service is particularly friendly or attentive, it's nice to leave a few coins or round up — about 5 percent is more than plenty. When paying by card, leave the tip in cash; there's usually no way to add it onto the card total.

For taxis, simply round up to the next euro. For example, if the meter reads €13, give them €14.

For other services — hotel staff, guides, or anyone providing a personal touch — a euro or so is a nice way to show appreciation. If someone's doing you a solid, a little tip is in order. There is a solution if you're clueless on whether to tip. Don't dwell on it — ask someone on the street or your hotel's staff, and don't worry about it. The intention is to be kind, not perfect.

Staying connected in Paris is easier than ever, but a little prep before your trip can save you time, stress, and money. Whether it's for navigating the city, booking tickets, or staying in touch with people back home, here's how to handle phone calls, data usage, and internet access while traveling.

International Calling Tips

If you need to make a call while abroad, how you dial depends on where you're calling from:

- **From a U.S. mobile phone**: Hold down the 0 key until you see a **+** sign. Then dial the **country code** (France is **33**) followed by the number (leave out the leading 0). Example: **+33 1 42 34 56 78**

- **From a U.S. landline to Europe**: Use **011** instead of the + sign, then dial the country code and number. Example: **011 33 1 42 34 56 78**

- **From a European landline to the U.S. or elsewhere**: Dial **00**, then the country code (U.S. is **1**, France is **33**) and the number. Example: **00 1 212 555 6789**

For full dialing help, visit https://www.howtocallabroad.com/.

How to use your Phone in Europe

International Plans

Before you leave, check if your mobile carrier offers a **global roaming plan**. Most U.S. providers (Verizon, AT&T, T-Mobile, etc.) have daily or monthly international options, including talk, text, and data. These are great for short trips or light phone usage and can be activated from your account settings.

Use Wi-Fi to Save Data

Many hotels, cafés, restaurants, and even parks and train stations offer free Wi-Fi. Take advantage of it whenever possible, especially when using maps, uploading photos, or making video calls. If you're in a public place, just ask for the **Wi-Fi password**—it's common and expected.

Reduce Mobile Data Use

Even with an international plan, try to limit data-heavy tasks like video streaming or cloud backups unless you're on Wi-Fi.

- **Download maps** offline using Google Maps before heading out.
- Use **WhatsApp**, **iMessage**, or other apps over Wi-Fi instead of SMS.
- Turn off auto-updates or background data for non-essential apps.

eSIM: A Digital, Hassle-Free Option

An **eSIM** is a virtual SIM card you install on your phone via an app—no need to remove your regular SIM. It's easy, quick, and ideal for short trips.

Popular eSIM providers include:

- **Airalo** – Affordable and reliable, with plans starting around $4.50 for 1 GB.
- **Holafly** – Best for **unlimited data** plans. Easy setup and strong coverage.
- **Nomad** – Offers flexible, pay-as-you-go-style plans and easy installation.

To use an eSIM:

- Make sure your phone is **unlocked** and **eSIM-compatible** (most newer iPhones and Androids are).
- Download the app, choose a France or Europe plan, and follow the setup instructions.
- Activate it once you land in Paris.

Physical SIM Cards: Traditional but Still Useful

If your phone doesn't support eSIM or you prefer something more familiar, you can buy a **prepaid SIM card** once you arrive.

Recommended options:

- **Orange Holiday Europe** – One of the best for tourists, includes 12 GB of data, calls, and texts across Europe.

- **SFR La Carte** – Flexible prepaid plans and decent network coverage.

- **Bouygues Telecom** – Reliable service and good data bundles for visitors.

You can buy SIMs at:

- **CDG or Orly Airport** – Look for Relay stores or Tourist Info desks.

- **Electronics stores** – FNAC, Darty, or Boulanger.

- **Supermarkets** – Carrefour, Auchan, or Monoprix often carry starter kits.

Bring your passport when buying a SIM—it's often required for registration. And double-check that your phone is **unlocked**, or the card won't work.

Final Tips

- **Turn off roaming** if you're using a local SIM or eSIM.

- **Always carry a backup**: either a printout or offline copy of key maps and contacts.

- **Know your PINs**: Some payment terminals or kiosks may ask for a 4-digit PIN, even with tap-to-pay cards.

- **Check compatibility**: Some budget phones may not support all network bands used in France.

Whether you choose an international plan, a local SIM, or an eSIM, staying online in Paris is simple—you just need to choose the method that fits your style and budget.

Resources from Adrian Nakamura

Planning a smooth and enjoyable trip to Paris doesn't just come from knowing where to go—it comes from preparing smartly, packing right, and learning from those who've been there before. Adrian Nakamura, a Paris-based guide and longtime transatlantic traveler, shares his approach to getting the most out of the City of Light.

He blends the instincts of a local with the practical sense of someone who's guided visitors from all walks of life. His suggestions, field-tested and flexible, are designed for travelers who want both comfort and freedom while exploring Paris.

Clothing

- 6 shirts, both long- and short-sleeved for layering options
- 3 pairs of pants, skirts, or capris—choose what suits your style
- 1 pair of shorts, ideal for warmer weather
- 6 pairs of underwear and socks for day-to-day comfort
- 1 pair of comfortable walking shoes, perfect for exploring on foot
- 1 warm layer (sweater or fleece)
- 1 lightweight, waterproof jacket with a hood
- Optional extras: scarf, belt, hat, or tie
- Swimsuit (for hotel pools or spas)
- Sleepwear or lounge clothes

Money

- Debit card(s) (with international access)
- Credit card(s) with no foreign transaction fees
- $100–200 in U.S. cash for emergencies
- Slim money belt or neck pouch

Documents

- Passport (valid for at least 6 months)
- COVID-related documents (vaccination proof, test results, etc., if required)
- Driver's license, student ID, or other helpful cards
- Copies of travel confirmations (flights, hotels, car rental, train tickets)
- Travel insurance info (print + digital)
- Guidebook or printed notes

- Notebook, pen, or a slim travel journal

Toiletries

- Toothbrush, toothpaste, floss
- Soap, shampoo, deodorant
- Hairbrush or comb
- Sunscreen and lip balm
- Travel-sized hygiene items

Health & Personal Care

- Prescription meds + basic first-aid supplies
- Contact lenses or glasses (plus backup)
- Sunglasses
- Reusable face masks and small hand sanitizer
- Magnesium citrate or other digestive aids

Extras

- Mini sewing kit
- Tissue packs (for public restrooms)
- Earplugs or travel earbuds for noise

Electronics

- Smartphone
- Charger (bring an extra cable if possible)
- Travel adapter (Type C or E for France)
- Headphones or earbuds
- Camera + accessories (if you're not just using your phone)
- Backup battery or power bank

Final Note from Adrian:

"You don't need much to enjoy Paris—but you do need the right things. Bring less than you think, walk more than you planned, and leave room in your bag—for bread, books, and whatever surprises the city has waiting for you." – *Adrian Nakamura.*

Helpful French Words

Knowing how sounds work in French can be hugely helpful even if you're just learning some vocabulary. In the next section I've also phoneticized the English to enable you to pronounce each phrase with more confidence. It won't take the place of listening to actual French speakers, but it will give you a strong place to start.

One quick tip on pronunciation: The French letter "j" is softer than the English version, leaning toward the "s" in "measure" rather than the "j" in "John." The final consonants are often silent, and the French "r" is pronounced from the throat. Relax, don't worry too much about making it perfect. For the French, a smile, a polite tone and a sincere effort can go a long way. If you want a complete breakdown of French sounds, I made an entire pronunciation guide that you can check out afterward.

Just a Note on "Tu" and "Vous"

French has two ways of saying "you": tu and vous. It can feel counterintuitive at first, but the rules are quite simple. Use vous when addressing someone you don't know, especially if they're your elder or if you're in a formal situation — for example, a shopkeeper, hotel staff or taxi driver. Use tu in kids, friends, or the people you close. In the examples I've listed, I've selected the form that best fits typical travel contexts. I provide both forms where both are common.

With talkative people, you can often hear tu es simplify into t'es in normal in everyday speech, same with tu as which would get shortened to t'as. It's not textbook French, but it's something you very commonly hear in conversations, and it's perfectly natural. I've listed a few of these forms so you know them if they arise. If you're interested in the looser side of the language, I've also a guide to everyday, slangy French expressions — perfect for understanding the locals and sounding a bit more able on the street.

Let's begin with greetings you'll hear every day in Paris. They're easy to remember and always appreciated by locals.

Bonjour (bon zhoor) means "hello" and is the standard greeting throughout the day.

Bonsoir (bon swahr) means "good evening" and replaces bonjour once it gets dark.

Salut (sa loo) is the casual version—similar to "hi"—used among friends or younger people.

Enchanté(e) (on shon tay) means "nice to meet you" and is commonly used when introducing yourself.

Keeping the Conversation Going

After greeting someone, a bit of small talk helps break the ice.

Ça va? (sa va) is the classic "How are you?" and can also be used to say "I'm fine," depending on your tone.

Ça roule? (sa rool) is a laid-back version of the same question, perfect for chatting with   friends.
Comment vas-tu? / Tu vas bien? (kommon va too / too va byan) are informal ways to ask how someone is.

Comment allez-vous? (Kommon Tally Voo) is the formal version, used with strangers   or   in   polite   settings.
Je vais bien (juh vay byan) means "I'm doing well."

Et toi? (ay twah) or **Et vous?** (ay voo) means "And you?"

Polite Words and Phrases

Being polite in French goes a long way. Here are some essential expressions of courtesy:

Merci (mair see) means "thank you."

Merci bien (mair see byan) is a slightly warmer or more polite way to say thanks.

Merci beaucoup (mair see bo coo) adds more enthusiasm—"thank you very much."

De rien (duh ryen) is the usual reply, meaning "you're welcome" or "it's nothing."

Excusez-moi (eh skyoo zay mwah) or **pardon** (par don) can both be used to say "excuse me" or to politely get someone's attention.

If you didn't hear someone say, say **Comment?** (Kommon?) or **Excusez-moi ?**, meaning "Sorry?" or "What was that?"

For a stronger apology, use **Je suis désolé(e)** (juh swee deh zo lay), which means "I'm sorry."

If you want to let someone pass or encourage them to go ahead, say **Vas-y** (va zee) for casual, or **Allez-y** (ah lay zee) in formal situations.

Phrases for Handling Problems

Sometimes, things don't go as planned, and it helps to know how to ask for assistance.

Pouvez-vous… ? (poo vay voo) means "Can you…?" and can be used in many ways.

Pouvez-vous le répéter, s'il vous plaît ? (poo vay voo luh ray peh tay, seel voo pleh) means "Can you repeat that, please?"

Pouvez-vous m'aider, s'il vous plaît ? (poo vay voo may day, seel voo pleh) is how to ask, "Can you help me, please?"

Je ne comprends pas (juh nuh kom pron pah) means "I don't understand."

Je n'ai rien compris ! (juh nay ryen kom pree) Means "I didn't understand anything."

Je ne parle pas (beaucoup) français (juh nuh parl pah bo coo fron say) lets someone know you don't speak much French.

Je suis perdu (juh swee pair doo) means "I'm lost."

Qu'est-ce que ça veut dire ? (kess kuh sah vuh deer) asks "What does that mean?"

Parlez-vous français / anglais ? (par lay voo fron say / on glay) means "Do you speak French?" or "English?"

If you're not feeling well, say **Je ne me sens pas très bien** (juh nuh muh son pah tray byan) or **Je suis malade** (juh swee ma lad) to say "I'm sick."

Fais attention! (fay ah ton sion) or **Faites attention !** (fet ah ton sion) means "Be careful!"

In case of emergency, shout **Au secours!** (oh suh koor), which means "Help!"

French Question Words

Even if you're just starting, learning a few key question words will help you ask for what you need—or understand what someone's asking you.

Quoi – What? *(kwah)*

Quand – When? *(kon)*

Qui – Who? *(Kee)*

Comment – How? *(kommon)*

Combien – How many? *(kom byan)*

Où – Where? *(oo)*

Pourquoi – Why? *(pour kwah)*

Quel / Quelle / Quels / Quelles – Which? *(kell)* — This one changes to match the gender and number of the noun that follows it, but it's always pronounced the same.

How to Ask in French

Now that you know the building blocks, here are some full questions you might use—or hear.

Comment tu t'appelles ? *(kommon too tappel)*

Tu t'appelles comment ? *(too tappel kommon)* Both mean "What's your name?" The first is a bit more formal, the second more casual.

Quel âge as-tu ? *(kel aj ah too)*

T'as quel âge ? *(ta kel aj)* These both mean "How old are you?"

Quelle heure est-il ? *(kel er eh teel)*

Il est quelle heure ? *(eel ay kel er)* "What time is it?" The second version is more common in conversation.

C'est combien ? *(say kom byan)*

Ça coûte combien ? *(sa coot kom byan)* Both ask "How much is it?"

Tu viens d'où ? *(too vyen doo)*

T'es d'où ? *(tay doo)* These mean "Where are you from?"

Tu comprends? *(too kom pron)* "Do you understand?" (Just raise your tone at the end.)

Tu parles anglais / français ? *(too parl ong glay / fron say)* "Do you speak English / French?" (informal)

Parlez-vous anglais / français ? *(parlay voo ong glay / fron say)* Same meaning, but this one is formal.

Où est la salle de bains ? *(oo eh lah sal duh ban)*

Où sont les toilettes ? *(oo son lay twah let)* Both mean "Where is the bathroom?"

Common French Responses

Here are useful phrases for sharing information about yourself or responding to basic questions.

Je m'appelle... *(juh mah pell)* – My name is...

Je suis... *(juh swee)* – I am... (used for name, nationality, job, etc.)

J'ai 30 ans *(Jay Tront on)* – I'm 30 (literally: "I have 30 years")

Oui *(wee)* – Yes

Non *(noh)* – No

Peut-être *(puh tetr)* – Maybe

Tout le temps *(too luh ton)* – All the time

Tous les jours *(too lay zhoor)* – Every day

Parfois / Des fois *(par fwah / day fwah)* – Sometimes

Jamais *(zha may)* – Never

Bien sûr *(byan sur)* – Of course (pronounce the "s" like an "s," not "sh")

Say It Right on Special Days

If you're invited somewhere or want to share good wishes, these phrases are perfect.

Amuse-toi bien! *(ah myooz twah byan)* – Have fun! (informal)

Amusez-vous bien! *(ah myoozay voo byan)* – Have fun! (formal)

Bon voyage! *(bon voy ahzh)* – Have a good trip!

Bonnes vacances ! *(bonn vah konce)* – Have a nice holiday!

Bon appétit! *(bon app uh tee)* – Enjoy your meal!

Félicitations ! *(fay leess ee tah sion)* – Congratulations!

Bienvenue ! *(byan vuh noo)* – Welcome!

Joyeux anniversaire ! *(zhwa yuh zahn ee vair sair)* – Happy birthday!

Joyeux Noël ! *(zhwa yuh no ell)* – Merry Christmas!

Bonne année ! *(bonn ah nay)* – Happy New Year!

French Farewells Made Simple

These are common ways to say goodbye in French, depending on the time of day or situation.

Au revoir ! *(oh ruh vwah)* – Goodbye

Bonne journée ! *(bonn zhoor nay)* – Have a good day

Bonne soirée ! *(bonn swah ray)* – Have a good evening

Bonne nuit ! *(bonn nwee)* – Good night

À bientôt ! *(ah byan toe)* – See you soon

À demain ! *(ah duh man)* – See you tomorrow

SIDEWALKS OF PARIS

Paris has long been regarded as the cultural core of Europe. This walk starts on the Île de la Cité the birthplace of Paris — and crosses to the Right Bank, leading you through centuries of history, from ancient Celtic roots to Roman rule, from medieval times and revolutionary zeal to the bohemian cafés of the 1920s, to the energy of modern-day Paris.

You'll pass by two of the city's most famous landmarks: Notre-Dame and Sainte-Chapelle. (Note: Notre Dame is still undergoing restoration from a fire in 2019, and you can currently only visit its exterior.) The complete walk is about three miles and could take four hours if you dawdle at every site along the way.

Take the time to linger over a lengthy lunch, enjoy a café crème, browse through a few antiquarian bookstores or simply watch the Seine float by.

Top Sight

Paris Passlib'

Several stops on this walk are covered by the Paris Passlib, which offers good value and allows you to skip the ticket line at all the major sites. The pass is available at the newsstand/gift shop at 5 Boulevard du Palais, directly opposite the entrance to Sainte-Chapelle.

Notre-Dame Cathedral

The world-famous cathedral has reopened to the public after being completely restored since a fire in 2019. There is no admission fee, but visitors must make a timed reservation, which is advisable to book online ahead of time to avoid long waits. Visitors can now enjoy the restored nave, chapels and altar, as well as newly designed liturgical furniture and new seating.

Daily from 8 a.m. to 6:45 p.m. (through 7:15 p.m. weekends).

Reservations via the official website are mandatory.

Address: **6 Parvis Notre-Dame – Pl. Jean-Paul II, 75004 Paris**, Métro: **Cité** or **Saint-Michel**

Website: www.notredamedeparis.fr

Sainte-Chapelle

This **Gothic masterpiece** is famous for its stunning stained-glass windows. Entry is **€11.50** for a timed ticket or **€18.50** when combined with the Conciergerie. It's also **included in the Museum Pass**. Booking ahead is highly recommended, as **on-site tickets are limited**. Open **daily from 9 a.m. to 7 p.m.** (closes at 5 p.m. from October to March).

Optional **audio guide: €3**

Address: **4 Boulevard du Palais**, Métro: **Cité**

Phone: **+33 1 53 40 60 80**

Website: www.sainte-chapelle.fr

Deportation Memorial

Located behind Notre-Dame, this **quiet, moving space** honors the memory of Holocaust victims deported from France. **Entry is free**, with optional **audio tours available** (45 minutes).

Open daily from **10 a.m. to 7 p.m.** (closes at 5 p.m. from October to March). Be aware of **occasional unannounced closures**.

Métro: **Cité**

Phone: **+33 6 14 67 54 98**

Conciergerie

This former royal palace and Revolutionary prison once held **Marie Antoinette**. Entry is **€11.50** or **€18.50** combined with Sainte-Chapelle. It's also covered by the **Museum Pass**. Open **daily from 9:30 a.m. to 6 p.m.**

Multimedia guide available for **€5**

Address: **2 Boulevard du Palais**, Métro: **Cité**

Phone: **+33 1 53 40 60 80**

Website: www.paris-conciergerie.fr

Tips to Beat the Crowds

This area tends to be the **busiest from late morning through mid-afternoon**, especially on **Tuesdays** (when the Louvre is closed and tourists shift here) and **weekends**. Try arriving **early in the morning** or visiting toward the **end of the day**. Lines at Sainte-Chapelle can be long due to its small size, and **security screening** can add to wait times. Early birds will have the smoothest experience—and a quieter one, too.

Let's Begin

Starting Point: Notre-Dame Cathedral

Your walk begins right in the heart of Paris—**Notre-Dame Cathedral**, located on the **Île de la Cité**, the historic center of the city. You're standing on a small island in the middle of the Seine, and from here, all of France quite literally spreads outward. The nearest Métro stations are **Cité**, **Hôtel de Ville**, and **Saint-Michel**.

As you take in the scene, notice the crowd of people from all over the world gathered in the square, **Place du Parvis**. Right in front of the cathedral, on the ground, is a small bronze marker known as **Point Zéro**—the official center of France. All distances in the country are measured from this exact spot. It's a symbolic and geographical heart—if Paris has a soul, it beats right here.

Notre Dame and Its Story Through Time

On **April 15, 2019**, flames tore through Notre Dame, destroying its roof and iconic spire. The world watched in shock as the cathedral burned. But that event was just one moment in a much longer story—a history that stretches back more than **2,000 years**.

In ancient times, this island was home to a small Celtic tribe called the **Parisii**. They fished, traded, and crossed the river at this exact point. When the **Romans** conquered the area in **52 BC**, they built a temple to **Jupiter** where Notre Dame now stands.

After the fall of Rome, the **Franks** took control and built a Christian church called **St. Etienne**. By the time **Charlemagne** was crowned emperor around **800 A.D.**, this site had already seen centuries of transformation. His statue still stands near the cathedral, reminding visitors of the early foundations of France.

In the **12th century**, a massive construction project began: the building of **Notre-Dame de Paris**. Over the next 150 years, stonemasons and laborers shaped what would become a Gothic icon. The result was a cathedral with **twin bell towers**, **flying buttresses**, and a now-lost **central spire** that once rose over 300 feet high.

By the **18th century**, during the French Revolution, Notre Dame fell into ruin. Revolutionaries destroyed statues, removed the spire for safety, and turned the cathedral into a storage warehouse. The square around it was crowded with medieval homes, and the building itself was in danger of being forgotten.

Then came **Victor Hugo**. His 1831 novel, *The Hunchback of Notre-Dame*, captured the public's imagination and brought attention back to the neglected cathedral. Thanks to the book's popularity, a movement grew to restore the building.

In **1844**, a young architect named **Viollet-le-Duc** took on the task. He led a full-scale Neo-Gothic renovation—adding the now-iconic spire, restoring the statues, and even adding those famous grotesque gargoyles. By the end of the 19th century, Notre Dame had become one of the most admired buildings in the world.

That was the version we knew until the fire in 2019. The rebuilding has since become a symbol of resilience and pride. As of **December 2024**, the doors are open once again—ready for a new chapter in the life of this legendary cathedral.

Below Your Feet: Layers of History

Beneath the plaza outside Notre-Dame lies **ancient Paris**—including Roman streets, medieval cellars, and the foundations of earlier churches. While most of it remains buried, a small portion has been excavated and is open to the public at the **Archaeological Crypt** just to the right of the cathedral entrance.

Now that you've explored the roots of Paris, take a moment to admire **Notre Dame** itself. Then, continue with the walk—it only gets better from here.

The Notre-Dame Front

Though the 2019 fire devastated the roof and spire, **the front façade of Notre Dame remains largely untouched**—a powerful symbol of endurance through centuries of upheaval. For now, let's focus on this extraordinary western face of the cathedral, which continues to impress visitors with its detail, scale, and symbolism. Notre-Dame means "Our Lady," and this church is dedicated to the Virgin Mary. At the center of the facade, above the main doors, you'll see a **statue of Mary holding the infant Jesus**, framed by the great **rose window** behind her. This central image has long represented **mercy, love, and refuge** for the faithful. If you look up—roughly two-thirds of the way up the **left tower**—you'll spot one of **Paris's most photographed gargoyles**. Try to get as close to the building as current access allows, and take a good look at the rows of **statues above the three doorways**. Each set tells a story carved in stone nearly 800 years ago.

St. Denis

On the left portal, you'll find a figure holding his head: **Saint Denis**, the patron saint of Paris. According to legend, he was beheaded by Roman soldiers for preaching Christianity. But the story doesn't end there—Denis supposedly **picked up his severed head**, washed it in a fountain, and walked until he found a place to rest. A church was later built on that spot, and he became one of France's most beloved saints. His image here stands as a testament to faith that refuses to be silenced.

The Last Judgment – Central Portal

Now step to the **main central doorway**, where carvings show a dramatic scene: the **Last Judgment**. Christ sits enthroned with both hands raised just beneath the pointed Gothic arches. Below him, an angel and a devil **weigh souls on a scale**—though the devil is cheating, pushing down to tip the balance. To one side, the saved look up toward heaven. On the other, the damned are chained together, being led off to a fate worse than waiting in line at the Louvre on a scorching August day.

The Kings of Judah

Look even higher—above the portals, under the central rose window—and you'll see a row of 28 stone figures: **the Kings of Judah**, ancestors of Christ. But there's more to the story. During the **French Revolution**, these statues were mistaken for French kings and seen as symbols of the monarchy and the Church's power. Revolutionaries climbed up and **chopped off every head**, shouting slogans and destroying what they thought were royal icons.

For more than a century, these figures stood **headless**, a visual reminder of revolution and ruin. Then, in **1977**, a schoolteacher digging in his backyard in Paris uncovered a remarkable find: the **original heads**, which he had buried for safekeeping during the chaos. Today, you can see those very heads on display at the **Cluny Museum**, just a short walk away.

More Than a Monument

Notre-Dame is not just a photo stop. For nearly a **thousand years**, it has been a place of **worship, protest, refuge, celebration**, and rebirth. Even if you don't step inside today, take a quiet moment to **stand in front of it**, breathe, and imagine the millions of lives that have passed through its doors.

Virtual Walk: Inside Notre-Dame

Let's step inside—virtually—for a moment.

Imagine entering through the great doors as a simple peasant might have centuries ago. You walk into a cool, dim space lit only by flickering candles and beams of light filtering through **vivid stained-glass windows**. The sound of **Gregorian chant** or

Mass echoes through the vast hall as your eyes follow the towering **columns** upward, stretching ten stories into the vaulted ceiling shaped like **praying hands**.

You walk the **central nave**, flanked by two side aisles. At full capacity, the cathedral could hold around **10,000 people**. Finally, you reach the **altar**—the heart of this cruciform church. Here, the faithful received communion, and for generations, this very spot has been sacred to **pagans, Christians, and even revolutionaries**.

During the French Revolution, all religious imagery was removed. In its place stood **mannequins dressed as Lady Liberty**, part of a national movement to replace religion with symbols of reason and liberty. Notre-Dame has seen it all—from ancient Roman temples to revolutionary firebrands to 21st-century crowds gathering for its rebirth.

As you circle the cathedral, it becomes clear that **Notre-Dame is not just a monument—it's a treasure house**, almost like Paris's own open-air Smithsonian. Inside its **Treasury**, safely tucked away, rests the **Crown of Thorns**—believed by tradition to be the very one worn by Jesus. Nearby, you'll find a gold-and-enamel **reliquary of Saint Geneviève**, the fifth-century patron saint of Paris, who is credited with saving the city from Attila the Hun through prayer and unshakable faith.

Elsewhere inside, a painting honors **Thomas Aquinas**, the 13th-century philosopher-priest who studied at the University of Paris and wrote some of the most influential works blending faith and reason. Not far from that, a statue of **Joan of Arc** stands tall. Once condemned as a witch and burned at the stake, she was later **canonized in this very cathedral**. Her presence here reflects the layers of history embedded in every stone.

The **north transept** houses the **blue-and-purple rose window**, one of the oldest parts of the church. Amazingly, it still holds its original medieval stained glass—though currently covered and protected during restoration. The newest visual feature is the massive **white tarp** stretched over the cathedral's roof, shielding the work in progress.

End your virtual visit with a pause at one of the quiet side **chapels**, where candles once flickered and prayers continue in silence. Even if you can't light one today, you can imagine the glow and look forward to the day when this place fully shines again.

Rue du Cloître-Notre-Dame

At the back of the cathedral, you'll find **public displays (in English and French)** that explain how the fire began, the rescue efforts, and the long road to restoration. One story that stands out: the **rooster-shaped weather vane** from the top of the steeple was found intact among the ashes—a small miracle and symbol of hope.

As you walk along, you'll also get a close-up look at some of the restoration work. **Gaps in the stained-glass windows** are noticeable—each pane is being tested for lead before being returned to place. **The flying buttresses**, those classic Gothic supports, are currently reinforced by large wooden frames. It's a rare moment to witness the behind-the-scenes work of preserving a masterpiece.

Keep walking a little farther, and you'll reach a new perspective. Just beyond the cathedral garden, cross over **Pont Saint-Louis** and take a detour...

Île Saint-Louis

If Île de la Cité is the city's historic anchor, **Île Saint-Louis** is its elegant neighbor—a quiet, refined residential island filled with **beautiful old buildings**, **boutiques**, cozy **bistros**, and **famous ice cream shops** like Berthillon. It's well worth a stroll, whether for a brief detour now or a longer return in the evening when it becomes peaceful and glowing under the streetlamps.

But for now, let's head to the Left Bank. With **Notre-Dame behind you**, turn to the **south side** of the cathedral and step into a small **grassy park** hidden just behind a tall green hedge.

Deportation Memorial

This powerful space is dedicated to **the 200,000 French victims** of **Nazi concentration camps** during the Second World War. After France fell in 1940, Paris spent years under Nazi occupation. **Jews, resistance fighters, and dissenters** were arrested, deported, and, in many cases, never returned.

As you descend into the memorial, the city disappears behind you. The noise fades. You're surrounded by cold stone walls—an intentional design meant to evoke the isolation of captivity. The narrow corridor is lined with **thousands of small crystal lights**, each one representing a lost life. At the far end, an **eternal flame** flickers quietly.

Above the exit is a stark inscription:

"Forgive, but never forget."

This memorial isn't long, but it stays with you.

Back on the surface, exit the garden and **turn left**. Walk to and across **Pont de l'Archevêché**. On the other side, you're now on the **Left Bank**. Turn **right along the river**, following Notre Dame's **southern edge**. We're now heading into one of Paris's most charming areas—let's keep walking.

The Artistic Side

Welcome to the **Rive Gauche**—the Left Bank of the Seine. It's called "left" because it's on your left-hand side when floating downstream. This part of Paris feels older, quieter, and more intimate. Narrow alleys, crooked buildings, and medieval charm still shape much of the area's layout.

While the **Right Bank** has modern offices, big boulevards, and Parisians in suits rushing to meetings, the Left Bank moves at a slower pace. Along the river, you'll see rows of green boxes mounted on the parapet—these are the **bouquinistes**, secondhand booksellers who've worked here since the mid-1500s. They open and close as they like and take pride in being unhurried, poetic, and just a little eccentric. For them, it's not just about selling books—it's about loving books.

Side View of Notre-Dame

Directly across from Notre-Dame, there's a **gap in the bookseller stalls** that leads to a staircase down to the riverbank. From here, you'll have one of the best views of the cathedral's side.

Before the 2019 fire, this view was dominated by **Viollet-le-Duc's tall spire**, lined with copper statues, and a green **lead roof** that gleamed in the sun. Those are now gone, as are most of the stained-glass windows—except for the three massive **rose windows**, which are currently covered for protection.

Even so, you can still see the full genius of the cathedral's **Gothic architecture**. It's all here: **pointed arches**, delicate **tracery** around the windows, dramatic **pinnacles**, ornate **rooftop sculptures**, and the grand **flying buttresses**—some of the most striking in the world.

These stone beams, reaching out from the building like arms, weren't just decorative. They carried the weight of the roof outward through the walls and down to the ground, which allowed builders to open up the walls for **stained glass**. That's the magic of Gothic design—engineering meets beauty.

Even the **gargoyles** had a job. Besides looking spooky and symbolic—souls stuck between heaven and earth—they also served as **rainspouts**, their open mouths channeling water off the roof. (That's where the word *gargoyle* comes from—the same root as "gargle.")

Imagine **Quasimodo** from *The Hunchback of Notre-Dame* hobbling across the roof among these beasts. This is the view he might've had.

Through Square Viviani

Once you're back at street level, walk in front of the cathedral to **Pont au Double**. Cross the bridge, turn left, and just ahead, you'll enter **Square Viviani**—a small park with benches and greenery. Look for a gnarled old **acacia tree** tucked inside. It's called the **Robinier**, and it's one of the oldest trees in Paris, planted in **1602**.

On the far side of the square stands **St-Julien-le-Pauvre**, a humble stone church with **Romanesque bones** and **Byzantine services**—one of the oldest in the city. Across from it, narrow **Rue Galande** cuts through what feels like a time capsule.

A Gothic church may take centuries to build, but legend says it only takes **thirteen tourists**: one spire, six columns, and six flying buttresses.

Paris in the Middle Ages

As you pass St-Julien-le-Pauvre, picture Paris around **1250 AD**. The city was alive with new energy. **Notre-Dame** was nearly complete, **Sainte-Chapelle** had just opened, and the **University of Paris** was attracting scholars from across Europe.

This neighborhood—stretching along **Rue Galande**—still whispers that medieval world. Look at the uneven rooftops, the way the buildings lean over the street, the small courtyards. People here once built wherever they could, pushing right up to the Seine, which served as Paris's main commercial artery.

It wasn't all romance and cobblestones. Imagine the **smell of fish**, smoke, sweat, and sewage. Families, merchants, fishmongers, bakers, and scholars all lived shoulder-to-shoulder in the tightly packed lanes.

Keep walking just a little farther. When you reach **Rue de la Bûcherie**, turn left— back toward the river and into the next chapter of this Left Bank journey.

Shakespeare and the Company

The **Left Bank** has always been home to writers, thinkers, and dreamers. Alongside medieval butcher stalls and fishmongers, it gave rise to Paris's literary soul. One piece of that legacy lives on in the quirky bookshop **Shakespeare and Company**, a shrine to books and bohemian life.

The original shop opened in the 1920s on **Rue de l'Odéon**, founded by **Sylvia Beach**, an American expat passionate about literature and freedom of thought. Paris, with its affordable rents and free-flowing wine, attracted the post–World War I **Lost Generation**—young Americans escaping prohibition, seeking culture and creativity. Her bookshop became their haven. **James Joyce, Hemingway, and Gertrude Stein** all gathered here.

Today's Shakespeare and Company is just across the river from Notre-Dame, still charming, still crammed with books, beds, and cats. From here, continue along **Rue du Petit-Pont**, turn onto **Rue Saint-Jacques**, once the Romans' main road through the city, and soon you'll reach **Saint-Séverin Church**, a fine example of late Gothic architecture.

Conciergerie

Next, we step into one of Paris's most somber and fascinating landmarks—the **Conciergerie**, once part of a royal palace, later a prison during the French Revolution.

Pick up a **free map** at the entrance and follow the suggested route. You'll start in the **Salle des Gens d'Armes**, where guards once ate beneath the low vaulted ceiling. Just beyond it, where Room 4 now houses a bookshop, stood the path known grimly as "**Monsieur de Paris**"—a nickname for the executioner.

Past the bookshop, you'll enter the **Office of the Concierge**, the official who processed prisoners—and sometimes gave them "last requests." Continue through the next cell, where **condemned prisoners** could wash and change before their final cart ride to the guillotine at **Place de la Concorde**.

A memorial room lists the names of **2,780 victims** executed during the Revolution. Some names, like **Robespierre, Charlotte Corday**, and **Louis XVI**, are defaced. But look closely, and you'll find **Marie-Antoinette** listed as "Capet Marie-Antoinette" on row 10.

A quiet **chapel**, hidden behind thick curtains, was built on the site of her final prison cell. Three simple paintings tell her story: saying goodbye to her children, receiving the sacraments, and her final moments before execution. Outside in the **Cour des Femmes**, women once walked in circles for air beneath the ever-present threat of death. Look up—you'll still see **iron spikes** along the walls.

On **October 16, 1793**, Marie-Antoinette left here in a cart and was taken to her death. The Conciergerie isn't just a museum—it's a haunting place where you feel history breathe.

When you exit, **turn left on Boulevard du Palais**. On the corner, look up to see **Paris's oldest public clock**, dating from **1334**. Then take another left onto **Quai de l'Horloge**, walking beside the Seine.

Place Dauphine

Tucked behind trees and facades, **Place Dauphine** is a quiet triangular square that feels more like a hidden village than a central Paris plaza. Cafés, benches, and the **Supreme Court building** (Palais de Justice) lend a dignified calm to the area. Check the "Eateries Along This Walk" section for a meal break here.

At the square's end, a statue of **King Henry IV** welcomes you. While not as famous as his grandson **Louis XIV**, Henry was crucial in shaping modern Paris—commissioning the **Pont Neuf**, this square, and laying the foundation for the city's future as a European capital.

Step onto the **Pont Neuf** and pause at the lookout point halfway across. It's a quiet spot with a view stretching down the Seine.

Pont Neuf and the Seine

Despite its name—**"New Bridge"**—**Pont Neuf** is the **oldest standing bridge in Paris**, completed around **1600** under Henry IV. It spans the river's widest point and was revolutionary in its time for being open—no houses were built on it, only **turrets** designed for vendors and performers.

From here, you can see the **Pont des Arts** pedestrian bridge downstream, the **Louvre Museum** on the Right Bank, and the **Orsay Museum** on the Left. In the far distance, the **black Montparnasse Tower** rises above the city.

This is where Paris began—on the Seine, which flows nearly **500 miles** from Dijon to the English Channel. Though calm and shallow through the city, the river once flooded regularly until the **stone embankments** were built around **1910** to control its power.

In summer, these quays transform into **Paris Plages**—pop-up beaches with sun chairs, umbrellas, and dancing locals. **Tour boats**, **barges**, and **fishermen** still glide past, following a rhythm older than the city itself.

You've reached the end of the walk, but it's not over.

From **Pont Neuf**, you can take a **river cruise** with **Vedettes du Pont Neuf** just below the bridge. To continue your journey, hop on the **Métro at Pont Neuf** or catch **Bus 69** nearby—eastbound on Quai du Louvre or westbound on Rue de Rivoli.

Wherever you go next, remember—you've just walked across more than 2,000 years of Parisian history.

And it's still unfolding.

THE LOUVRE MUSEUM

The Louvre is more than a museum — it's a cross section of the artistic arc of the Western world. It is an overwhelming but unforgettable experience with more than 30,000 works of art. You won't see everything in a single visit, so in this guide, I'll focus on a few highlights that are essential to the Louvre experience: the Greek sculptural collections, Italian masterworks, and French painting.

From prehistoric bas-reliefs and the enduring lucency of the Venus de Milo to the dynamic rage of the Winged Victory of Samothrace, you'll trace evolving conceptions of beauty through time. You'll meet peaceful medieval Madonnas, the inscrutable Mona Lisa, and grand works that honor elements of democracy and revolution. You'll learn a lot about what people believed in, what they valued, and what they dreamed about by looking at what different civilizations admired.

Essential Info

Opening Hours

Open **Wednesday to Monday**, **9:00 a.m. to 6:00 p.m.**

Closed on **Tuesdays**.

The last entry is 45 minutes before closing.

Note: On **Wednesdays and Fridays**, hours may be extended into the evening—check the official website for current details.

When to Visit

The museum is busiest on **Sundays**, **Mondays**, and **weekday mornings**. If you can, opt for an **evening visit**, which is usually much calmer.

Renovation Notices

Be aware that certain galleries or rooms may close for maintenance or renovation. Room numbers and layouts can also change, so stay flexible during your visit.

Tickets and Prices

Standard admission: **€17**, timed-entry ticket (online purchase recommended). Included in the **Paris Museum Pass**

Your ticket includes access to temporary exhibitions, but reentry is not permitted once you exit the secured areas between the museum wings.

Entry Requirements & Reservations

You still need to reserve a timed entry in advance, even as a holder of a Museum Pass. That said, same-day reservations occasionally open up, but to ensure you get your desired time it's best to book at least one day in advance.

How to Get In Without a Reservation

If you arrive without a ticket or reservation (which isn't recommended), you may still be able to buy a €15 timed-entry ticket on site—though only during slower periods. For last-minute sales, head to the side room beneath the glass pyramid.

If you do require a Museum Pass, proceed on foot to La Civette du Carrousel, a small tabac (tobacco shop) located within the Carrousel du Louvre underground mall. It sells the Museum Pass at its requested value (cash only). Inside the mall, follow signs for "Museum Pass."

Métro Access

The closest Métro station is **Palais Royal–Musée du Louvre**. From there, follow the signs to the **Carrousel du Louvre** underground entrance or walk directly to the pyramid entrance above ground.

By Bus

Take **Bus No. 69** along the Seine:

- **Eastbound**: Get off at **Quai François Mitterrand**, just before the museum.

- **Westbound**: Get off right in front of the Louvre's **glass pyramid** entrance.

Taxi

A taxi stand is on Rue de Rivoli, near the Palais Royal–Musée du Louvre station.

Bike Rentals

There are several Vélib' stations nearby if you're coming by bike — a simple, eco-conscious way to navigate central Paris.

Louvre Entrances

Most visitors enter through the dramatic glass pyramid in the courtyard holding the main entrance. If you've already reserved your timed-entry ticket, you can skip the long lines to purchase tickets and head straight to security instead.

The underground entrance at 99 Rue de Rivoli, known as the Carrousel du Louvre, is a quieter and often faster option. This entrance leads directly to the Métro and the Carrousel du Louvre shopping mall. Look for signs for "Musée du Louvre — Le Carrousel du Louvre," and head toward the inverted pyramid. Skip the detour set up for general visitors — it's longer and often more crowded.

Tours and Audio Guides

English Guided Tours usually depart from under the pyramid at Accueil des Groupes, normally at 11:00 a.m. and again at 2:00 p.m., particularly during peak seasons. Tours last about 90 minutes.

Advance online booking is smart (cost: €12 plus museum admission) or +33 1 40 20 52 63.

Want a more self-guided experience? Rent a multimedia guide for €5. It includes more than 700 works of art, and offers useful commentary on the major exhibits.

Plan to spend at least 2 hours there, but longer is better if you can swing it.

Facilities and Amenities

Lockers

Only small daypacks are allowed in the galleries. Keep your things in the free self-service lockers in the pyramids' underbelly.

Restrooms

Most bathrooms are located below the pyramid, too. There are limited facilities within the museum wings themselves, so plan accordingly.

Dining Options

If you are looking for lunch options inside and around the Louvre:

- **Café Mollien**: At the tour's end, with terrace overlooking the pyramid.

- **Bistrot Benoit**: An upscale alternative beneath the pyramid.

- **Richelieu Wing Cafeteria**: Quick and casual, self-service dining accessed by escalator.

- **Carrousel du Louvre Food Court**: On the upper mall level, fast-food and grab-and-go.

Must-See Highlights

You won't see it all, but do stop for these essentials:

- Venus de Milo

- Agamemnon's Mask

- Mona Lisa

- Works by **Leonardo da Vinci, Michelangelo, Raphael** and major French masters

Tackle the Louvre

The **Louvre** is a sprawling U-shaped palace and the **largest museum in the Western Hemisphere**. Navigating it isn't easy, but that's part of the adventure. The building is divided into three main wings:

- **Richelieu Wing** (north): Near Eastern antiquities, decorative arts, and Northern European painting (including German and Dutch masters).

- **Sully Wing** (east): Home to French paintings and extensive collections of **Egyptian** and **Greek antiquities**.

- **Denon Wing** (south): Where you'll find many of the museum's most famous works—**Italian Renaissance art**, **ancient Greek sculpture**, and **French Neoclassical and Romantic painting**.

For this visit, we'll focus mainly on the **Denon and Sully Wings**, where the greatest hits live. Just be aware: the Louvre is massive and constantly evolving. Rooms might close temporarily, numbers may change, and artworks are sometimes loaned out or under restoration. Focus on the highlights and conserve some energy—you'll need it.

Getting Started

Enter through the **main glass pyramid**, descend into the lobby, and head toward the **Denon Wing**. Take the **escalator up one level**. Show your **ticket** at the checkpoint, then walk forward about **25 steps** and take the **first left**, following the signs marked **Antiquités Grecques**. Keep going until you reach **Room 170**, under a low brick ceiling labeled **Grèce Préclassique**.

Pre-Classical Greece – 3000 B.C.

This section features early Greek art—**simple, solemn, and still**. The first glass cases display figures carved more than **a thousand years before the Egyptian pyramids**. These **Cycladic figurines**, often likened to abstract dolls, represent women with their features stripped down to the bare essentials—long noses, folded arms, and stylized bodies.

Further down the gallery, you'll spot the **Dame d'Auxerre**, a small limestone statue representing feminine dignity and composure. Next to her stands a **Kore figure**—rigid and upright, hands at her sides, with blank eyes and a faint smile. These early statues weren't about motion; they were about **stillness, order, and presence**.

That would soon change. By **450 BC**, Greece entered its **Golden Age**, a time of intellectual and artistic explosion. Sculpture became more fluid, more human, more alive. Artists began to seek balance—between energy and serenity, motion and rest. You'll see that shift with one of the ancient world's most celebrated works...

Venus de Milo (Aphrodite)

At the end of the pre-classical section, exit and climb **one more flight of stairs**. At the top, turn **left** (think 11 o'clock), pass through a **domed gallery**, and enter the **Sully Wing**. After walking about **50 yards**, take a **right** into **Room 345**.

There she is: **Venus de Milo**, standing tall above a crowd of admirers. Found in **1820 on the Greek island of Melos**, this statue instantly became a sensation across Europe. By the 19th century, the Western world was already obsessed with classical antiquity, and Venus seemed to capture its essence.

She is also known as **Aphrodite**, the goddess of love and beauty. Her body—curved, proportional, graceful—represents **the Greek view of harmony and cosmic order**. The Greeks believed their gods looked like humans because **human beings, in their ideal form, reflected divinity**.

Though her arms are lost, Venus still stuns viewers. Not with power or action, but with **poise, balance, and timeless elegance**.

Venus de Milo: A Closer Look

Stand in front of her, and try this: **split Venus vertically down the middle.** You'll see how each half mirrors the other in balance and grace. She stands in a classic

contrapposto pose—her weight on her right leg, left leg slightly raised, setting her whole body in motion.

That subtle shift causes her **right shoulder to dip** and her **head to turn** in the opposite direction, forming an elegant **S-curve**—seen not just from the front but from the back as well. It's quiet motion captured in stone.

Her upper body is smooth and polished, contrasting with the **rough texture of her lower half**, where her garment—carved in thick, heavy folds—clings to her body. Look closely: Venus was carved in **two separate blocks of marble**, joined at the hips (you can still see the seam). Her face blends realism and idealism—recognizably human, yet too flawless to be anyone in particular. She isn't a person—**she's an idea**: the Greek ideal of womanhood.

And the arms? They're long gone. Some say she raised her **left arm**, perhaps holding an apple or crown, while the **right** tugged gently at her robe. Others imagine her leaning on a pillar or embracing another statue. Personally? I think she was **picking lint out of her belly button**—but that's just me.

Take your time to walk around her. **Every angle reveals something new.** Her back has just as much life and form as her front. When you're ready, follow her gaze into the next part of the gallery.

The Gallery of Statues

Now, look around this long hall filled with **Greek sculpture**—an homage to the human form at its most refined. Here, art moves beyond symmetry and stiffness. From around the **5th century BC**, Greek artists learned how to portray **natural movement**. The classic **contrapposto stance**—where the figure's weight rests on one leg while the other is relaxed—offered a perfect blend of motion and stillness.

In this gallery, you'll find **gods, warriors, athletes, satyrs, and civilians**—each rendered with a balance between divine ideal and everyday reality. Many statues once held **spears**, **shields**, or **helmets**, now lost to time. But the postures and expressions endure.

One highlight here is a towering **statue of Athena**, goddess of wisdom and war. She stands opposite Venus de Milo—**wisdom facing beauty**—clad in armor, calm but ready to defend Athens. Artists of the Golden Age weren't just celebrating gods—they were exploring the tension between **human imperfection** and **divine ideals**.

The Parthenon Friezes – Salle 347

Now backtrack slightly and enter **Salle 347 (Diane Room)**—to the **right of Venus**, about 30 yards back. This room houses original **relief panels from the Parthenon**, created in the mid-5th century BC at the height of Athens' power.

On each wall, you'll see **two large marble slabs**, once mounted on the **Parthenon's outer walls**. The small **architectural model** in the center of the room shows exactly where these carvings once hung. For example, the **centaur panel** may have stood over a doorway, while the **procession of young women** would have been displayed just below the roofline. (To get the full effect, crouch and look up at the model.)

One relief depicts a **centaur attacking a woman**, symbolizing chaos and barbarism. But look closely: the humans fight back, representing **Athens overcoming foreign threats**, especially the Persians.

On the opposite wall, a more peaceful image: **young girls in ceremonial dress**, walking in a sacred procession. Every year, they offered a **hand-embroidered shawl** to the 40-foot statue of Athena inside the Parthenon. Here, in just a few inches of marble, the **flow of fabric**, the **grace of posture**, and the **stillness of tradition** are all captured. Their skirts fall in stiff vertical lines like **fluted columns**, but their arms and legs break free—**stone becoming human**.

Look at the central male figure—his torso relaxed, his arm flexed, **veins visible** in the stone. He isn't posing—he's alive. This is what made Greek art revolutionary: **form meets soul**.

Roman Detour (Rooms 409–418)

Before moving on, take a short detour into **Salle 409**—the beginning of the **Roman Antiquities** section. Backtrack about 20 feet from Venus de Milo and turn into this hallway filled with marble stares and imperial egos.

Here, you'll meet the **faces of Rome**—the Caesars and their families—captured in stone and frozen in posture. Look beyond their stoic expressions and try to glimpse the personalities behind them. Some are **"Emperor Inconnu"** (literally "Unknown Caesar"), while others are unmistakable.

There's **Augustus**, Rome's first emperor—composed and almost godlike—and his calculating wife **Livia**, who made sure her son **Tiberius** inherited the throne. Tiberius, by the way, is the Caesar mentioned in the **"render unto Caesar"** line in the Bible.

Next, you might spot the deranged stare of **Caligula**, the cruelty of **Domitia**, or the bearded wisdom of **Hadrian**, who turned beards into high fashion. Finally, the marble eyes of **Marcus Aurelius**—the philosopher-emperor—seem to gaze right through you as if trying to stay calm while Rome burned from within.

While Roman **engineering and warfare** were groundbreaking, their art was often practical and imitative. They didn't try to outdo the Greeks—they just **copied** them. Many of the sculptures here are **replicas** of Greek originals, made to decorate Roman villas, temples, and public buildings. Still, their **portrait busts** are distinct—hyperrealistic, sometimes harsh, often unflattering—designed to show power and mortality, not divine perfection.

Winged Victory of Samothrace (c. 190 BC)

Keep walking through the Roman halls until you reach a **staircase**. At the bottom, look up—and you'll see one of the **Louvre's most stunning works**: the **Winged Victory of Samothrace**.

She stands at the top of the stairs like she's about to **take flight**. The setting—a prow of a ship, the wind in her garments—isn't just dramatic. It's **theatrical**. Originally placed high on a cliffside on the island of Samothrace to commemorate a **naval victory**, she embodies movement, tension, and triumph.

Her robes whip around her body, **clinging and twisting** in ways that suggest water, wind, and battle. Her wings are flung back, her torso leans forward, and though she's missing both arms and her head, you feel the **momentum**. She doesn't need them.

Unlike the ideal calm of Venus de Milo, **Victory is all energy**—raw, windblown, unbalanced, and alive. She's a product of the **Hellenistic period**, around 190 BC, when art became more expressive and emotional. Where earlier Greeks aimed for still perfection, these artists captured **struggle and motion**.

And her hand? In 1950, archaeologists found what's believed to be her **right hand**, open and raised. Unfortunately, it was in **Turkey**, and when France asked for it back, negotiations went as expected. Let's just say Turkey didn't raise one finger—they raised **the** finger.

Above You: Icarus and the Louvre Pyramid

Facing Victory, glance up. In the **Octagon Room**, the sculpture of **Icarus** dangles dramatically from above—like he's about to crash through the ceiling. Look out the nearby window for a striking view of **I.M. Pei's glass pyramid**, one of Paris's most iconic (and once controversial) landmarks.

The Louvre as a Palace

It's easy to forget that the Louvre was once a **royal palace**. Over **700 years**, kings expanded it, redesigned it, and eventually lost it. The **Sully Wing**, just behind you, sits on the foundation of a **medieval fortress**. The **Tuileries Palace** once stood 500 yards west, beyond the Arc de Triomphe du Carrousel, where the pyramid's open courtyard now spreads.

Through centuries of renovations, the Louvre's wings slowly reached toward one another, finally forming a full rectangle by **1852**. But the **Tuileries Palace burned down in 1871**, after just 19 years of use, during a violent uprising. Its ruins were cleared, but the Louvre remained.

In 1989, architect **I.M. Pei** unveiled the **glass pyramid**. Locals hated it—just like they'd hated the **Eiffel Tower** a century earlier. Today, it's beloved. Give it time— Paris always comes around.

Beneath the dome of the Octagon Room, look for a plaque reading:

"Le Musée du Louvre, fondé le 16 Septembre 1792."

After the **French Revolution**, the Louvre was transformed into the **first public museum in Europe**. The monarchy was gone, and with it, the private world of royal collections. The people claimed the palace, opened its doors, and declared art a right, not a privilege.

A fitting monument to a city that never stops reinventing itself.

The Apollo Gallery

Step into the **Apollo Gallery,** and you step into the mindset of **absolute monarchy**. This is what royal grandeur looked like before **Louis XIV** built Versailles. Picture the scene: gilded walls, ornate stucco ceilings, candlelit evenings, and conversations about myth, power, and glory under the watchful eyes of France's legendary rulers.

The space is lined with **tapestries and paintings**, mixing French historical figures with scenes of mythological or symbolic importance. Decorative objects—**crystal vases**, **marquetry furniture**, and intricate tableware—reflect the wealth and ambition of a country that, for centuries, led Europe in both art and politics.

Look for portraits of famous French kings:

- **Henri IV**, builder of the **Pont Neuf**

- **François I**, the king who invited **Leonardo da Vinci** to France and brought the Renaissance with him

- **Louis XIV**, the **Sun King**, elevated royal spectacle into an art form

At one end of the gallery, glass cases house part of the **French Crown Jewels**. The display changes occasionally, but you might see:

- Crowns used by **Louis XV**

- The modest but significant **Crown of Charlemagne**

- And the dazzling **Regent Diamond**—a 140-carat stone once worn by **Louis XVI**, **Napoleon**, and others. The jewels reflect not just power but the mythology of monarchy—the belief that kings ruled by divine right and were themselves living symbols of the state.

The Medieval World (1200–1500)

Not far from the Apollo Gallery—just past **Salle 650**, near the **Sully Wing**—there's a rare and much-appreciated **toilet** (WC). But from here, to continue with the art, retrace your steps toward **Winged Victory**, cross the central hall, and head into the **Denon Wing** to **Room 706**.

In here, you'll see two **frescoes by Botticelli**—early examples of how the artistic spirit of **ancient Greece** was rediscovered in the **Italian Renaissance**. But before diving into that world, let's rewind to where it all came from: the art of the **Middle Ages**.

Continue into **Salle 708**, and you're back in a time when **faith ruled Europe** and art was its messenger. From around **1200 to 1500**, Europe was shaped by the **Catholic Church**, which offered order and hope in a world that felt dangerous and unstable after the fall of Rome.

Nearly every European church had its **altarpiece**—a central devotional image that often showed **the Virgin Mary**. During this period, Mary was the most adored figure in Christianity, more venerated than any saint and more beloved than even Jesus in some ways. She was the human link between the divine and the ordinary, and people prayed to her with deep devotion.

Altarpieces from this era followed a familiar formula:

- **Flat gold backgrounds**, meant to symbolize heaven

- **Rigid, iconic figures**, arranged with symmetry and serenity

- **Elegant drapery** and stylized angels—pure, holy, and remote from human flaws

One master of this style was **Cimabue**, whose work feels like cutouts from another dimension—hovering on gold leaf, spiritual and untouchable.

Giotto: St. Francis of Assisi Receiving the Stigmata

(c. 1295–1300)

Just ahead, you'll encounter a turning point.

In **Giotto's** painting of **St. Francis of Assisi**, you can feel the shift from medieval abstraction to Renaissance realism. The scene is quiet and powerful: Francis, a humble monk, kneels on a **rocky Italian hillside**, gazing up at a vision of **Christ with six wings**. Beams of light shoot from Christ's wounds and strike Francis on the **hands, feet, and side**—the **stigmata**, mirroring Christ's crucifixion.

Here, the mystical becomes human. Giotto doesn't flatten the figures or blur the emotion—he brings the vision **down to earth**, showing Francis as a real person in a real place, having a deeply spiritual but personal experience.

This is where art begins to change. Inspired by Francis's message of **compassion, nature, and humility**, Giotto and his contemporaries began to paint real people in real spaces, expressing **real emotions**. The **Renaissance** is still decades away, but the seeds are here.

This is how beauty, spirit, and humanity began to reconnect in Western art. And now, you're about to follow that thread into the full bloom of the Italian Renaissance.

Giotto: Painting in the Present Tense

Giotto di Bondone (c. 1266–1337) doesn't just tell stories—he **directs them**. He stops time at the most powerful instant, much like a film director freezing the action at its peak. His works don't aim for realism in a technical sense, but they **feel real**—as if we're witnessing the moment unfold in slow motion.

Take his **St. Francis Receiving the Stigmata**. The perspective is clumsy by modern standards—Francis's hut is smaller than he is, and Christ somehow faces us while reaching toward Francis—but that's beside the point. Giotto creates **layers of space**: the saint in the foreground, the hut in the middle, and the rocky hillside behind. The scene becomes **a stage**, and we are its audience.

At the bottom edge of the panel—called the **predella**—you'll spot **birds gathered at Francis's feet**, waiting as if they, too, know a sermon is coming. Giotto brings us into a world where **divinity meets nature**, and humans stand somewhere in between.

The Italian Renaissance (1400–1600)

Now move into the **Grand Gallery**, a long, majestic hallway built in the late 1500s to connect the **old Louvre palace** with the now-lost **Tuileries Palace**. Today, it holds one of the Louvre's most celebrated collections: **Italian Renaissance paintings**.

From the entrance, look down the length of the gallery. It's long. So long that walking it in under **two minutes in heels** might earn you a small medal (or a twisted ankle). Try if you like—but more importantly, take your time to **spot the traits** that define this period:

- **Symmetry**: Madonnas often sit at the center, flanked by saints like bodyguards
- **Realism**: Faces look familiar—these aren't icons; they're people
- **Three-Dimensionality**: Vast landscapes stretch into the background
- **Religious Themes**: Madonna and Child, martyrs, saints everywhere
- **Classical Influence**: Greek gods and poses sneak into Christian art—Mary might look like Venus, but her virtues are all Christian

Leonardo da Vinci — *The Virgin and Child with St. Anne* (c. 1510)

Here, **Leonardo** builds a perfect **triangle** of three generations—**St. Anne**, **Mary**, and **Jesus**—arranged in a graceful pyramid. Anne, the grandmother, anchors the base. Mary, sitting on her lap, reaches to the side. Baby Jesus leans playfully forward, turning away as he wrestles a lamb.

One foot points left. One arm reaches right. A body twists upward. **It should feel chaotic**, but it doesn't—it's peaceful, ordered, and somehow serene. Leonardo gives motion to the moment, but **his geometry keeps it grounded**, like a universe governed by divine symmetry.

Raphael — *La Belle Jardinière* (c. 1507)

Just a few steps down, you'll find **Raphael's** luminous **Madonna in a garden**, surrounded by **the infant Jesus** and **John the Baptist**. Like Leonardo, he arranges the figures into a soft triangular shape—but his style is more delicate, more graceful.

Mary gazes down at Jesus with gentle love. He reaches up toward her while standing in a miniature **contrapposto**, as if practicing for Greek sculpture. John kneels at Jesus's feet, holding a small cross—a quiet symbol of the sacrifice to come.

The three interact through **gestures and glances**, giving the painting a sense of **warmth and unity**. Raphael's brushstrokes are so smooth they almost glow, blending form and light into something ethereal.

With Raphael, the **Renaissance ideal of beauty** reaches its peak. After him, many tried to imitate it—sometimes too sweetly, with **sugarcoated Madonnas** that lack his spark. But here, in this painting, you see why his genius was so admired: it's not just beautiful—it **feels complete**.

Leonardo da Vinci — *Mona Lisa* (1503–1506)

A short walk brings you to **Salle 711**, home of the most famous face in art: **Mona Lisa**—or as the French call her, *La Joconde*. She sits alone, encased in glass, set against a freestanding wall. You'll know you're close not by a sign but by the **buzz of the crowd**—the only painting in the Louvre that you can hear before you see. (You might even smell it if the room's full.)

When **Leonardo da Vinci** moved to France at the invitation of **King Francis I**, he brought only a handful of paintings. Among them was this portrait of **Lisa del Giocondo**, the wife of a wealthy Florentine merchant. Francis was so taken with the work that he made it a centerpiece of his royal collection, which eventually became part of the **Louvre Museum**. In Italian, she was called *La Gioconda*, a play on her last name and the word for "joyful." We call her *Mona Lisa*—short for *ma donna Lisa*, or "my lady Lisa."

What You Might Not Expect

If it's your first time, the painting might surprise you. She's **smaller than expected**, darker, and set back under thick glass. She looks like a quiet secret in a loud, cavernous room. So why all the fuss?

Well, love doesn't always meet expectations. If you're going to adore her, **you have to meet her as she is**, not as you imagined.

That Smile

Start with the **smile**, the one that's launched a thousand theories. Leonardo used a technique called **sfumato**—literally, "smoky"—blurring the edges of her mouth and jaw so finely that it's hard to tell where one ends and the other begins. Her expression shifts depending on where you stand, how you feel, and what light hits the surface. Is she happy? Sad? Mocking? Tired? In love?

The truth is, **she's not telling**—and that's the magic. She reflects your mood at you. She's a kind of emotional mirror, a **Rorschach test in oil paint**.

The Details That Make It Work

Her body rests in **perfect balance**, forming a subtle **pyramid** that stabilizes the composition. Her right arm rests calmly on a chair arm just at the edge of the frame, while her hands—calm, relaxed—fold together in her lap.

The **landscape behind her** is pure Leonardo: winding rivers, twisted paths, and mountains dissolving into mist. As the land recedes, it becomes more blurred, more dreamlike. It feels both **endless and unreachable**, like something remembered from a dream you can't quite place.

Her skin looks like **sculpted marble**, her clothing soft and fluid. There's a **veil** over her hair—barely visible to the naked eye, but detected through scans—which may suggest this was a **post-childbirth portrait**, a common tradition of the time. Others have speculated wildly: that Mona Lisa was **Leonardo in disguise**, or a mix of male and female features, or simply **an idea**—not a person.

Stillness, Secrets, and a Glance

What makes her powerful isn't her beauty but her presence. Mona Lisa isn't bold or loud. She doesn't command attention. She just **waits**—and that calm confidence is what draws you in.

She's **serene**, **measured**, and **distant**, like music drifting out of a metro tunnel—beautiful, but never quite yours. If you're patient, she might reward you with a quiet wink.

She won't give everything away. But she'll stay with you long after you leave the room.

Paolo Veronese — *The Marriage at Cana* (1562–1563)

Before you peel yourself away from the *Mona Lisa*, **turn around**. On the opposite wall sits **the biggest painting in the Louvre**, and one of the easiest to overlook—*The Marriage at Cana* by **Paolo Veronese**.

Step back ten paces. Let the whole scene fill your field of view. Then pause—because suddenly, **you're not just looking**. You're **invited**. This isn't just a biblical story; it's a party. So go ahead—**grab a glass of wine**.

The scene is full-blown Renaissance fantasy: **hundreds of guests, colorful robes, music, food, chaos**, and **elegance**. There are jesters, waiters, nobles, servants, pets, and even a couple of **misbehaving animals**. A man in yellow pours wine in the foreground. A cat and dog fight under the table. You'll find a **lion** too. And somewhere, almost lost in the crowd, is a **bride and groom**, far off to the left.

In the center—calm, detached—is **Jesus**, about to perform his first miracle: **turning water into wine**. But here, he's barely noticed. It's as if Veronese is saying: **divine or not, this man belonged to us—he was one of us**. A Venetian, a guest at our table, part of our celebration of life and beauty and indulgence.

It's **religious**, yes—but filtered through **Renaissance Venice**, where pleasure and faith mingled freely.

Now exit Mona's gallery and head through **Salle Denon (Room 701)**. On your **left** is a room filled with passion and drama—**French Romanticism**. But first, we look **right**, to one of the Louvre's most grand and self-important rooms: **French Neoclassicism**.

French Painting (1780–1850)

Here, **Napoleon** takes center stage—**literally**.

Born to modest parents, this self-made general didn't just want to be king—he wanted an **Empire**. In 1804, at **Notre-Dame Cathedral**, Napoleon seized his moment. With the pope watching, he took the crown and placed it on his head.

That scene is captured in **Jacques-Louis David's** towering masterpiece: *The Coronation of Napoleon*. It's more than just a historical record—it's a **propaganda bomb** in oil paint.

Look closely: Napoleon is about to crown **Josephine**, his first wife. And in the background, standing upright in a ray of light, is **Napoleon's mother**... who wasn't even at the ceremony. She had refused to come—but Napoleon had David **paint her in anyway**. Power rewrites the past.

David was Napoleon's official artist and unofficial **image-maker**. He didn't just paint—he **orchestrated**. He designed entire public ceremonies and made neoclassical style the visual language of French power: **clean lines**, **heroic poses**, and a love for all things **Greek and Roman**.

Look up at the balconies. On one, you'll spot **David's self-portrait**—gray curls peeking out from behind a tassel, as if even he couldn't believe what he was witnessing.

Jean-Auguste-Dominique Ingres — *La Grande Odalisque* (1814)

As you head back toward **Salle Denon**, stop at **Ingres's reclining nude**. It's like a **Venus de Milo turned horizontal**.

At first glance, *La Grande Odalisque* is classic: a lounging woman, delicate pose, smooth curves. But her body doesn't quite add up. Her back is impossibly long, her spine stretches like rubber, and her gaze is cool—almost bored.

Ingres wasn't aiming for anatomical accuracy. He wanted **elegance**, **rhythm**, and a sense of **dreamlike eroticism**. The woman is a fantasy, not a portrait—a blend of **Orientalism** and **idealized beauty**, filtered through a very French imagination.

Théodore Géricault — *The Raft of the Medusa* (1819)

While **Neoclassicism** prized order and intellect, **Romanticism** exploded with emotion. At its height in the early 19th century, Romantic art didn't whisper—it **screamed**.

Géricault's *Raft of the Medusa* is a perfect example. It's massive, muscular, and unflinchingly raw. The canvas shows a raft full of twisted bodies—men barely alive, clinging to hope, while corpses hang limp in the waves. At the right, a greenish body slumps overboard. On the left, a man cradles another's lifeless form, his face hollowed by starvation and despair.

This isn't fiction—it happened. In 1816, a French ship named the *Medusa* wrecked off the coast of Africa. The crew abandoned 150 people on a makeshift raft. After 12 days of starvation, madness, and **cannibalism**, only 15 survived.

Géricault, just 27 years old, set out to **shock France awake**. He interviewed survivors, studied corpses in morgues, and visited asylums to **capture real suffering**. His goal wasn't beauty. It was true.

But even amid horror, there's a **glimmer of hope**. The figures at the top of the raft form a pyramid, with one man waving frantically at a tiny rescue ship on the horizon. In a storm of despair, Géricault leaves us with the idea that **we might still be saved**.

Eugène Delacroix — *Liberty Leading the People* (1831)

Just a few years later, Paris erupted again—this time in **revolution**. King **Charles X** had imposed harsh restrictions. The people rose, and in 1830, they ousted him.

Delacroix, known for drama and color, didn't just paint the revolt—he **personified it**.

Liberty Leading the People captures the spirit of that revolution. **Liberty herself**, bare-breasted and fearless, charges forward with a **tricolor flag** in one hand and a musket in the other. Around her are all types of rebels: a working-class man with a sword, a bourgeois intellectual in a top hat, and a young boy—gun in each hand—ready to fight.

Delacroix's colors—**red, white, and blue**—aren't subtle. They're a national cry: **Liberté, Égalité, Fraternité**. She's part myth, part symbol, and completely human.

This painting is more than a tribute to one uprising. It's a visual anthem for **freedom**, still pulsing with energy nearly two centuries later. It belongs in the **Louvre**, a museum founded not for kings but for the **people**.

Now, pass **Café Mollien** and take the stairs down. There's one last stop waiting.

Michelangelo — *Slaves* (1513–1515)

These two marble statues—*The Dying Slave* and *The Rebellious Slave*—are among the few **Michelangelo sculptures** outside Italy. And they feel both **ancient** and **timeless**.

The *Dying Slave* leans back as if asleep or surrendering to music only he can hear. His pose is gentle but sensual—muscles relaxed, head tilted, skin smooth. His face, though unfinished, suggests peace. Some say this is Michelangelo's most **erotic** sculpture. It's certainly one of his most human.

The *Rebellious Slave*, by contrast, is all tension. His head twists one way, his body another. He fights against the stone, pushing to break free. Michelangelo believed that each sculpture already existed within the marble—that it was the artist's job to **release it**.

And here, you feel that struggle. The slave fights not just against his bonds but against the block itself. It's a metaphor for every creative act: the pain of shaping something out of resistance—and the beauty that emerges from it.

End of Tour

These statues may remain forever bound in marble, but you're free to go. Your walk through the **Louvre** has taken you across **thousands of years**, through empires, revolutions, gods, saints, lovers, kings, rebels, and myths.

Now it's time to step back into the real world—through the **Sortie** (exit) signs, down the stairs, and out into Paris. But don't be surprised if some of what you've seen stays with you.

Because once you've walked with **Mona**, **Victory**, and **Liberty**, it's hard to forget.

.

THE EIFFEL TOWER

Yes, it's crowded. Yes, it was expensive. And yes—**you should still go**.

There are other viewpoints in Paris, maybe even better ones. But nothing quite matches the feeling of standing on the **Eiffel Tower**. Unlike the Mona Lisa, which some say is smaller than expected, the Eiffel Tower never disappoints. It's **huge**, it's iconic, and even in a world of modern skyscrapers, it still holds magic.

You only get one chance to do this for the first time. The climb (or elevator ride) gives you that rush—**you're one of millions** who've made the pilgrimage to this symbol of Paris. Over 250 million people have visited it since it was built. And no matter how many times you've seen it in photos, **the real thing always hits differently**.

Quick Essentials

- **Price**:
  - **€27** for elevator access to the summit

- o **€17.50** for elevator to 2nd floor

- o **€11** for stairs to 1st or 2nd floor

- o **€21** for combo (stairs + elevator to the summit)

- o **The Museum Pass does not cover it**

- **Opening Hours**:

  - o **Mid-June to August**: 9:00 to 00:45

  - o **September to mid-June**: 9:30 to 23:45

  - o Last elevator ride **up**: 22:30

  - o **Stairs close earlier**—last entry around 18:30

  - o Can **close temporarily** due to wind at the top, but ticket holders may still access lower levels

  - o **Official site**: www.toureiffel.paris/en

Ticket Tips

Reserve ahead if possible.

Elevator tickets should be booked in advance to avoid long waits. Online tickets let you **skip the line** and choose your entry time. They usually open **60 days ahead**, around **8:30 a.m. (Paris time)**. They sell out fast from **April through September**, so plan early.

If summit tickets are gone, **book for the 2nd floor**—the views are still amazing. Also, check the site again a week before your visit—sometimes slots open up.

Note: **Stair tickets** are only sold on-site, not online.

No reservation? Here's what to do.

You can still try your luck, but be smart about it. Arrive **30 minutes before opening** to get through security and join the ticket line early. Or go in the **evening**, when the crowds thin out. After **7 p.m.** (May–August) or after **5–6 p.m.** in the off-season is often quieter. In winter, keep in mind that it gets dark by 5 p.m., which can make for a beautiful nighttime view.

Best timing:

Try to arrive while it's still light out so you can enjoy the full **panoramic view** of Paris. Stick around for **sunset and nightfall**—the tower lights up, the city sparkles below, and the whole experience feels magical.

Getting There

The Eiffel Tower is easy to reach from several directions.

- **Métro**: Take line 6 to **Bir-Hakeim** or line 9 to **Trocadéro**. Both are about a 10-minute walk.

- **RER C**: Get off at **Champ de Mars—Tour Eiffel** station.

- **Bus**: Lines **42, 69**, and **86** stop nearby.

- **Walking**: From Rue Cler, it's a 20-minute walk via **École Militaire** station.

Entry Process

Security First

The tower is surrounded by clear glass security walls. Entry is free to the base, but **everyone must go through airport-style screening**. This can take 30+ minutes during peak hours—factor that into your timing.

If You Have a Reservation

Arrive at least **30 minutes before your time slot**. After security, follow the **green signs** for **"Visiteurs avec Réservation" (Visitors with Reservation)**.

No Reservation?

After passing through security, look for the **yellow signs** pointing to **ticket booths** marked "Individuels" or "Visiteurs sans Tickets." If you're doing stairs, go to the **south pillar**, which is marked.

Tour Duration

- **With reservation + light crowds**: Plan for **90 minutes** if you're only heading up and down quickly.

- **Without reservation or during busy times**: Budget **3–4 hours** to go up, enjoy the views, and come back down—especially if you're aiming for the summit.

Safety & Bag Restrictions

- **No large bags** are allowed. If your bag is bigger than **48 × 20 × 30 cm (19" × 8" × 12")**, you won't be allowed in.

- **No luggage storage** is available on-site.

Facilities

- **Restrooms**: Free toilets are available at ground level behind the **east pillar**. There are also restrooms inside the tower on all levels, but expect **long lines** during busy hours.

Food & Drinks

Restaurants

There are two upscale restaurants inside the tower, both offering spectacular views. Dining there lets you **skip the ticket line** but not security. You can't enter more than **15–30 minutes before your reservation**.

- **1st Floor**: *58 Tour Eiffel* — modern French dining Phone: +33 1 72 76 18 46

- **2nd Floor**: *Le Jules Verne* — high-end gourmet restaurant Phone: +33 1 45 55 61 44

Picnic Option

Skip the price tag—grab food near **École Militaire** and head to **Champ de Mars park**. There are benches and grassy areas perfect for a picnic, but the central lawn is often off-limits. Aim for the sides.

Don't Miss

The Views

No matter how many photos you've seen, the views from the Eiffel Tower still manage to take your breath away. From up here, **Paris unfolds in every direction**—a perfect grid of rooftops, monuments, and bridges stretching to the horizon.

Viewing Platforms

There are **three levels** for visitors:

- **First level** (~200 feet): Less crowded, good views, glass floor section, exhibits, restrooms, shops.

- **Second level** (~400 feet): Often considered the **best viewpoint**—you can see major landmarks clearly without being too high.

- **Summit** (~900 feet): Windy, but offers an unbeatable **360° panorama**. You'll also find **Gustave Eiffel's private office,** restored here, and a champagne bar.

Each level has **toilets, souvenir shops,** and **informational displays**.

Climbing the Stairs

If you're up for it, you can **walk up to the second level**.

- **360 steps** to the first floor

- Another **360 steps** to the second That's 720 total steps you'll feel in your legs—but the sense of achievement is real. The stairs are **enclosed in mesh** for safety, but if you have vertigo, it can still be a bit dizzying.

The Full Experience

To experience the Eiffel Tower:

1. **Start at the base**, admire its scale up close.

2. **Go up to the second level**—either by stairs or elevator.

3. From there, **take the second elevator to the summit** (there is no direct elevator from the ground to the top).

4. Spend time at the summit, then **return to the second level** to explore the view again—this time, a bit more grounded.

5. If you're up for it, **descend by foot** and stop at the **first level**, where there's a glass floor, a small museum, and more displays.

6. Walk back down to the ground and look up—it feels different now.

The Tower from the Outside

From afar, the Eiffel Tower looks delicate and graceful. But up close, it's a **massive iron machine**, bold and unapologetically industrial. It stands **1,063 feet tall**, including its antenna—just slightly taller than the Chrysler Building in New York. That's about **77 stories**. Despite being made of **7,300 tons of iron**, it's engineered so efficiently that the pressure at its base is less than that of a linebacker walking in cleats.

Once the tallest structure in the world, it's since been passed by giants like:

- **Tokyo Skytree** – 2,080 ft

- **KVLY-TV mast** (North Dakota) – 2,063 ft

- **Burj Khalifa** (Dubai) – 2,717 ft

Surroundings

Just south of the tower is Champ de Mars, a long grassy park once used for military training. It's now a popular picnic spot. To the north, across the Seine, lies Trocadéro, with its wide steps, fountains, and one of the best photo spots in the city.

Lifts and Steps

The tower from the beginning included elevators — an engineering feat at the time, particularly because the legs of the tower do not sit vertically. Modern lifts now do around 100 round trips daily, and although there are 1,665 total steps, visitors can only walk up to the second level (720 steps).

For your info: When it was timed in 1905, a race from bottom to second floor took 3:12. Your pace may vary.

The importance of the history

The Eiffel Tower first towered over Paris for the 1889 World's Fair. It was constructed in celebration of the 100th anniversary of the French Revolution, a mass act of defiance, and in order to demonstrate to the world that France was still a daring, contemporary nation. As people walked through the base of the tower and into the fairgrounds they were walking into the future — beneath a structure taller than anything that had ever been built at the time.

A bridge engineer named Gustave Eiffel had won the competition to design the tower. His competitors had suggested ideas including a massive guillotine, but Eiffel's concept was distinctive. He evolved from merely an engineer to the key force behind the entire project. He financed most of it himself, manufactured the components in his factory and even invented machines to do the work. He remained intimately engaged throughout and finished the tower ahead of schedule and under budget.

The Eiffel Tower, you should know, wasn't always supposed to be there. It was meant to come down after twenty years. But the connection to it was forged quickly among Parisians. With the exception of some early criticism (the author Guy de Maupassant is said to have hated the tower so much that he preferred to eat lunch in it, just so he wouldn't have to look at it), it slowly became a beloved symbol of the city it came to define.

The tower has had many uses over the decades. It started transmitting radio signals in the early 1900s. It was used for cosmic-ray research in 1910. From 1925 to 1934, it famously hosted a giant lit "CITROËN" advertisement. During the 1940 Nazi occupation of Paris, it transmitted television signals for the German regime. In the wake of the war, it was home to fireworks, light shows and major events. Its current twinkling display was commissioned in 2000 to mark the new millennium.

Climbing to the Top

No visitor ever forgets getting to the top of the Eiffel Tower. And after climbing up or taking an elevator to the second level, you transfer to another elevator that brings you up to the summit — almost 900 feet up in the air, above the rooftops of Paris. On bright days, it offers views of up to 40 miles in each direction.

There are helpful viewing panels that label all the visible landmarks at the summit. (If you're looking west, you'll see a small replica of the Statue of Liberty standing on the banks of the Seine.) It looks at the original in New York City, more than 3,600 miles away. That's also appropriate because Gustave Eiffel was also responsible for the internal structure of the Statue of Liberty in the United States, conceived by French sculptor Frédéric Bartholdi.

Building the Tower

Picture the scene in 1887: Paris abuzz with excitement and workers starting to build something unlike anything the world had known. The Eiffel Tower was made of 18,000 iron pieces, all made off site, then brought on site and bolted together with 2.5 million red-hot rivets. As many as 300 men worked on the tower at its peak. Some balanced on narrow beams, unhooked from their harnesses, and others hung from rope ladders, hammering every rivet home one at a time. They started at the lower levels, propped up by wooden scaffolding. The legs angled inward, slowly converging at the top to form the tower's graceful silhouette.

Special steam-driven cranes, designed by Eiffel himself, were built on tracks that essentially moved upward along with the tower. Construction of the Eiffel Tower was completed in a little over two years. It rose more than 1,000 feet — taller than the Washington Monument — to become the tallest man-made structure in the world.

The tower was opened on May 15, 1889. At the top glowed a beacon in red, white and blue that night. It was not only an engineering success — it was a sign of progress and a statement to the world from a country proud of its role in modernity.

Originally a rusty red, the Eiffel Tower went through shades of mustard yellow before it settled into the brown-gray color it has now. It gets repainted by hand every seven years — a task that consumes 25 full-time painters and about 60 tons of paint.

As a temporary competition attraction and global beacon Admire it as you stand below it, or look out from its summit, and its part in the tale is undeniable.

Facing North (Nord)

Looking north, you can see the broad arc of the Trocadéro colonnade at your feet. This plaza was the site of the 1878 World's Fair and still provides one of the best frontal views of the Eiffel Tower. Beyond it is the Bois de Boulogne, a huge wooded park that draws joggers in the daytime and, how can I put this, a different type of clientele at night. In the distance, the familiar outline of La Défense, entered by its glass towers and corporate offices. At the opposite end of the Champs-Élysées, just to the right of Trocadéro, is the Arc de Triomphe, the other end point of the famous boulevard.

Facing East (Est)

Turn your gaze east, the river Seine guides your eye past a succession of handsome bridges. The most elaborate is Pont Alexandre III, distinguished by four gilded statues. Keep scanning upstream, to see the Orsay Museum and the Louvre and farther upstream, the Pont Neuf, with its twin towers of Notre-Dame Cathedral. In the distance, a dome atop a hill to the north — Sacré-Cœur atop Montmartre — looms like a white bullet above the city.

Facing South (Sud)

From the south, the Champ de Mars unfolds below, a green carpet to the École Militaire. Nearby, the Y-shaped UNESCO building rears up and, farther out, the dark shape of the Montparnasse Tower soars nearly 700 feet. To the left, in sunlight, you'll see the gleam of the golden dome of Les Invalides, which contains Napoleon's tomb.

The Summit

Climb a few last steps, and you will come to the very top of the tower — right under the antennas and satellite dishes. This is where Gustave Eiffel used to maintain an apartment, still recreated today with wax figures of Eiffel and inventor Thomas Edison, who famously presented Eiffel with one of the first phonographs. (No, they didn't play The Who's "I Can See for Miles," but it's a lovely image.)

Second Level – 400 Feet

And this is where you'll find the best panoramic views of Paris. It's easy to recognize landmarks at this altitude, and the city feels so close that you could touch it. There are souvenir shops, toilets and a small café. And where Michelin-starred Le Jules Verne, a fine dining restaurant helmed by Frédéric Anton, resides — ideal for those wishing to savor while soaring through the sky.

First Level – 200 Feet

This round, however, provides a much closer and similar experience. There's a small museum, theater and seasonal pop-up activities, such as playgrounds and even a ice-skating rink in winter. There's also a café and restaurant, as well as room to roam and absorb.

Don't skip the glass floor — a heart-thumping photo op that gives you the disorienting sensation of floating 200 feet in the air. It's a hit for selfies and goggle-eyed children.

One exhibit explains that thermal expansion can cause the top of the tower to shift as much as five inches toward the sun. That gentle action you might experience during strong winds is entirely by design — Gustave Eiffel built the tower with a little flex, to bend rather than break.

Getting Down

To leave, use the stairs or elevators. The stairs are generally faster (especially if you're going down) and provide a last opportunity to observe the structure's details from within its metal frame. It's a five-minute descent from one level down to the next — or, 360 steps.

Return to Street Level

Once you're down, please take it slowly. You can cross the Seine to visit Place du Trocadéro for a traditional postcard view or kick back in Champ de Mars park down the south side. The Eiffel Tower is impressive by day, but it is pure magic at night.

At night, the tower glows in warm gold — and once every hour, it twinkles for five minutes, flooding the sky with light. It's a good time to just stop, breathe and allow Paris to be what it does best: dumbfound you.

EXPLORING RUE CLER

A walk down **Rue Cler** is like stepping into the rhythm of daily Parisian life. This narrow, pedestrian-friendly street is more than a food market—it's the heartbeat of the neighborhood. Though the city continues to evolve, Rue Cler remains grounded in everyday traditions. Here, the French *art de vivre* is not a tourist performance but real life. Locals stop for fresh produce, linger over their coffee, and greet shopkeepers by name. It's all so ordinary—and that's exactly what makes it extraordinary.

Wandering Rue Cler

Start at the **north end**, where Rue Cler meets Rue de Grenelle (just a short walk from the **École Militaire Métro station** or the **#69 bus stop**). The best time to come is during **market hours**:

Tuesday to Saturday, 8:30 a.m. – 1:00 p.m. and 3:00 p.m. – 7:30 p.m.

Sunday morning until noon. Closed Sunday afternoon and all day Monday.

Give yourself at least **an hour** to browse, shop, and sit at a café. It's just a three-block walk, but full of charm. For tips on how to shop like a local, see the "Shopping" section in the Activities chapter.

Café Roussillon

Begin with a coffee at **Café Roussillon**. Sit outside or stand at the bar for cheaper prices—locals often do. This corner café buzzes with neighborhood life: kids wobbling on scooters, dogs on leashes, neighbors sharing a chat. Ground-floor shops and upper-floor apartments give the area that typical Parisian mix of residential and retail. Rue Cler is a community. Even if you're just visiting, you're part of it while you're here.

Check the chalkboard menu for wines by the glass, or simply sip an espresso and watch the city move.

Petit Bateau

Across the street, **Petit Bateau** offers stylish baby clothes, known especially for their classic sailor stripes. In France, children are often dressed with as much care as adults. The popularity of stores like this reflects a broader trend: France now has one of Europe's highest birth rates. Fashionable little ones are everywhere.

Au Bon Jardinier – "The Good Gardener"

Keep walking and cross **Rue de Grenelle** to reach **Au Bon Jardinier**, a local produce shop bursting with color. Their fruits and vegetables arrive fresh each morning from **Rungis**, the vast wholesale market just outside Paris. Want to blend in? Bring a canvas bag or a rolling cart—Parisians avoid plastic.

Locals buy what's in season and choose by scent. Sniff a French **Gariguette** strawberry, then compare it to an imported one—you'll understand why they call the Belgian variety "plastic." Check the back bins for fresh herbs or whatever's just come in. This is the kind of shop where the clerk may remind you what's best today... and what's not worth it.

Next door, you'll find a **Franprix**, a small supermarket, and just across from the **Grand Hôtel Lévêque** is **Traiteur Asiatique**, a popular Asian takeaway spot. These quick, affordable meals—noodles, rice dishes, dumplings—have quietly reshaped lunch habits in Paris, sitting comfortably alongside baguettes and charcuterie.

Wine Bacchus

A few doors down from the Grand Hôtel Lévêque, you'll find a small, well-curated wine shop called Wine Bacchus. Wines are arranged by region, which matters in France—many Parisians like to drink wines from where they or their family come from. You'll find quality bottles, with many good options under €12, especially from the monthly specials. The staff can help you pick the right bottle for your picnic or dinner, and if you choose white wine, they'll chill it for you in a few minutes using a "Le Chiller."

Café Évolution

This cozy café used to be a tobacco shop. Now, it's the kind of place where you can sit with a drink or a light snack and watch the street go by. It reflects how Rue Cler has shifted over the years—from a working-class market street to something a bit trendier. Some longtime locals miss the old, practical shops, but places like this still manage to hold on to that relaxed neighborhood feeling.

Fromagerie

Right next to the wine shop, the unmistakable scent of cheese leads you to the fromagerie. With over 200 varieties, including cow's milk, goat's milk, and sheep's milk cheeses, this shop is full of character. In France, these shops are often called *crémeries* or *BOF* stores—short for beurre (butter), œufs (eggs), and fromage (cheese).

Cheeses come in all shapes—discs, pyramids, cylinders—with various molds and rinds. The shape and look often point to where they're from, and the French are serious about terroir—the mix of soil, sun, and tradition that shapes the flavor. In the back room, giant wheels of cheese sit aging, weighing over 170 pounds each. It's worth browsing slowly. In restaurants, a cheese plate is often served right before dessert—or instead of dessert altogether.

Poissonnerie

Across the street is the fishmonger. Fresh fish is delivered daily from the coast, often so fresh it rivals what you'd find in seaside towns. Like other fish shops in Paris, it's spotless and neat, meeting EU hygiene rules but also pleasing picky Parisians.

À la Mère de Famille

A few steps away is a delightful chocolate and candy shop, À la Mère de Famille. This shop has been part of the neighborhood for decades. Inside, you'll find old-school and modern sweets—everything from chocolate bars to individually priced truffles. You can mix and match a custom box or just grab one or two treats to snack on. The owner says older customers still come in for the same sweets they've loved since childhood.

Former Boucherie Chevaline

Just next door, look for the charming storefront with stained glass and a mosaic sign that still reads *Boucherie Chevaline*—a reminder of when this shop used to sell horsemeat. It doesn't anymore, but the building hasn't changed. It's part of the old Paris you'll find hiding in plain sight.

Charcuterie-Traiteur Jeusselin

Down the block, there's a small building with two dormer windows on the roof—Rue Cler's oldest. The ground floor is home to Jeusselin, a beloved charcuterie-traiteur. Inside, you'll find award-winning cured meats, pâtés, sausages, roast chickens, and ready-to-eat dishes. These shops are lifesavers for Parisians with tiny kitchens. Many locals grab side dishes here to go with simple homemade meals. Just across the street is Davoli, Jeusselin's friendly rival. Both shops offer great takeaway options, especially before lunch and dinner. Roast chickens are hot and ready around 11:00 a.m. and again after 5:00 p.m.—perfect for a picnic in the park. To order, just pick your dish, pay at the cashier, and return with your receipt to pick it up.

Artisan Boulangerie

Bread is sacred in France, and this bakery keeps that tradition alive. The law says a *boulangerie* must bake its bread on-site, and here they do it well. Locals know exactly how they like their baguette—some prefer it dark and crusty, others more tender and pale. This spot does both. Even better, they've mastered pastries too, something most bakeries can't pull off equally. Stop in for a warm croissant or a just-baked *pain au chocolat*—you won't regret it.

Café du Marché and More

This café on the corner is the soul of Rue Cler. It's where locals gather, not just to eat but to catch up, unwind, and feel part of the neighborhood. The owner has purposely kept prices low so locals can enjoy dining out regularly—some even come five nights a week. If you're after an affordable meal, snag a spot on the terrace and take a look at the chalkboard for the daily special. The sidewalk tables are often full, thanks to France's non-smoking laws making outdoor seating more appealing than ever.

Just across the street is Aldi, a modern grocery chain focused on bulk shopping. Though it sticks out architecturally, it fills a practical niche. Still, many locals avoid it— tiny Paris apartments don't allow for bulk buying, and daily shopping for fresh produce and bread remains the norm. That's the rhythm of Rue Cler.

Turning right at the café, walk two doors down Rue du Champ de Mars, and you'll come to a little gem of a store...

L'Épicerie Fine

This gourmet shop is run by Pascal and Nathalie, a warm couple who love introducing travelers to French food culture. They make things easy with labels and explanations in English, and the shelves are full of elegant treats—artisanal vinegar, truffle oil, jams, fancy chocolate, and Berthillon ice cream. It's an ideal stop for gifts or picnic supplies, and it gives you a taste of the pride locals take in good food.

Near the intersection on Rue Cler, you'll often spot a small crowd gathered outside the corner bakery, waiting patiently for their turn.

Glacier Martine Lambert

Next door to Jeusselin, don't miss the little ice cream shop. Many Parisians say it's the best in the city. Whether you want one scoop or three, it's a sweet way to end your walk through Rue Cler.

Mephisto Shoe Store

A little farther down, the Mephisto shop blends into the flow of the street but serves a specific need. In a city made for walking, quality shoes are essential. These French-made shoes are known for comfort, and they're usually cheaper here than in the U.S. It's a quiet reminder that Parisians may be stylish, but they're also practical. Most people walk everywhere—to the market, the metro, the café—so good footwear isn't a luxury; it's part of everyday life.

Cler Fleurs and the Butcher Shop

On the opposite side of the street, Cler Fleurs adds a bright burst of color to the neighborhood. Since most Parisians don't have yards, flowers are a small but important luxury. You'll see window boxes and balcony pots overflowing with blooms—especially in spring and summer. Buying fresh flowers for the home is part of the rhythm of Parisian life.

A few doors away, the local butcher shop keeps an older tradition alive. The chalkboard lists out cuts of beef (*boeuf*), veal (*veau*), pork (*porc*), and lamb (*agneau*), usually sourced from French farms. It's a fading art, though—many younger people are moving away from the profession or meat altogether. Still, this shop stands as a link to the deep culinary culture that values every ingredient and every part of the animal.

City Info and Street Details

At the end of Rue Cler, where it meets the busier Avenue de la Motte-Picquet, there's a small digital display about ten feet off the ground. It flashes updates about local events, transport changes, job postings, and city initiatives. Nearby, you'll also spot a tall glass container for bottle recycling and translucent trash bags. These changes date back to the 1990s, after a series of bin bombings pushed the city to adopt more transparent—and safer—waste systems.

The Neighborhood Tabac and Cigar Cave

Across the avenue, there's a classic *tabac*, officially known as *La Cave à Cigares*. These little shops are the only places where you can legally buy tobacco in France. More than that, they're neighborhood hubs where locals buy stamps, metro tickets, lottery slips, and sometimes just pop in for a chat. You might spot graphic warnings on cigarette packs—EU regulations require them. Inside, there's also a humidor with a small stash of quality cigars. If you're curious, this might be the moment to pick up a petit Cuban as a souvenir.

Pharmacy on the Corner

Next door, the pharmacy fills an essential role in daily life. In France, pharmacists act as the first stop for minor health issues. They're trained to give medical advice and can even issue prescriptions for simple problems. For travelers, it's a great place to pick up basics—from cold meds and pain relievers to band-aids and travel-size toiletries.

End of the Walk

If you've collected picnic supplies along the way, you've got two excellent picnic spots nearby. For a quieter setting, turn left on Avenue de la Motte-Picquet and look for the small green park near the Army Museum. To go bigger, turn right instead and head straight to the Champ de Mars, where you can spread out on the grass beneath the Eiffel Tower.

When you're ready to head out, the École Militaire Métro station is just a short walk down Avenue de la Motte-Picquet—on your right as you leave.

THE GRAND CHÂTEAU OF VERSAILLES

Versailles was the grand finale of French royalty—a place built to impress. The name itself has come to mean "look at this," and it lived up to it. For nearly a century, Versailles was the cultural and political heart of Europe, with its court under Louis XIV setting the tone for style, art, and power across the continent. Much of what we associate with "French elegance" today has roots right here.

A visit to Versailles includes three main highlights. First is the **Château**, the main palace, where French kings once lived in over-the-top luxury. Inside, you'll find grand halls, crystal chandeliers, gold-framed mirrors, and rooms that once held royal secrets. Outside, fountains and statues line perfectly manicured gardens that stretch far into the horizon.

Then there were the **Trianon Palaces**, smaller but still refined retreats that offered a break from court life. Finally, don't miss the **Domaine de Marie-Antoinette**, where the queen tried to escape palace formality in her private world of meadows, cottages, and her own dreamy Hamlet—beautiful, yes, but also a bit sad.

Versailles is more than a palace—it's a story about ambition, power, beauty, and eventually, downfall.

Quick Information

Cost and Reservations

To visit the Château, you need a *timed-entry ticket*. You can book your slot for free on the official Versailles website. You can also buy tickets at Paris Tourist Information Centers or FNAC department stores (there may be a small service fee). If you're using the **Paris Museum Pass**, see the next section for how to reserve your time slot.

- **Château only**: €18
- **Passeport ticket** (includes Château, Trianon, and Domaine): €20
- **Passeport on Garden Show days**: €27
- **Trianon/Domaine only**: €12
- **Free entry**: First Sunday of the month, November–March

All tickets include a free audioguide.

Gardens

The gardens are open daily but *may require a separate ticket* on special "Spectacle" days (musical fountain shows). These usually happen on **Tuesdays, Fridays, Saturdays, and Sundays** from April to October. Entry to the gardens is *free* the rest of the week and from **November to March**.

Opening Hours

- **Château**:
    - April to October: Tuesday–Sunday, 9:00–18:30
    - November to March: Tuesday–Sunday, 9:00–17:30
    - The last entry is 45 minutes before closing. Closed Mondays.
- **Trianon/Domaine**:
    - Same hours as Château, but opens at 12:00
- **Gardens**:
    - Daily from 8:00 to 20:30 (April–October)

o   Close around 18:00 in winter

Getting There

To reach Versailles, hop on the RER C (Train C) from stations like Champ de Mars, Pont de l'Alma, Invalides, Musée d'Orsay, St-Michel, or Gare d'Austerlitz. The journey takes about 35 minutes southwest from Paris.

- Buy a **4-zone Navigo Day Pass** or a round-trip RER ticket to **Versailles Rive Gauche/Château** (approx. €7.20 round-trip).

- When you arrive, exit the station, turn right, then left onto the main boulevard, and walk 10 minutes straight to the palace.

Using the Paris Museum Pass

The pass gives free access to the **Château, Trianon Palaces**, and **Marie-Antoinette's Domaine**, but *not the gardens on Spectacle Days*. Even with the pass, you must reserve a **time slot online** in advance (look for "Palace ticket" on the Versailles website).

Buying Tickets in Versailles

If you arrive without tickets, expect lines. Before heading to the main entrance, check online for any last-minute availability. You can also buy tickets at the **Versailles Tourist Information Office** (near the train station). Guided tours are sometimes available there or through GetYourGuide. Worst case, line up at the palace's main ticket office (on the left side of the courtyard).

Crowd-Beating Strategies

Versailles gets extremely crowded, especially during the high season. To avoid the worst of it, try not to visit on holidays, Sundays, Tuesdays, or Saturdays. The best days are Thursdays and Fridays. The longest security lines form between 10:00 and 12:00 in the main courtyard, where you'll go through two separate checkpoints—one at the entrance gate and another before the palace itself.

Planning Your Time

To get ahead of the crowds, leave Paris around 8:00 a.m. This should get you to the gate just before it opens at 9:00. Start with the Château interior tour in the morning, followed by lunch around midday. In the afternoon, visit the Gardens and, if you have the time and energy, the Trianon Palaces and Domaine de Marie-Antoinette. These take about 90 minutes to explore, plus a 30-minute walk each way from the main Château, so if you're short on time, skip them.

Tours

Guided tours are available in English and last about an hour and a half. They include extra rooms that aren't on the general admission route and allow you to bypass the main security lines. The cost is around €10, and reservations can be made online or through Versailles's ticketing partners.

Garden Shows (Spectacles)

From April to October, the gardens host special musical events. One of the most popular is *Les Grandes Eaux Musicales*, which combines baroque music with the display of 55 fountains throughout the gardens. It takes place on Saturdays and Sundays from 11:00 to 12:00 and again from 15:30 to 17:00. From May through June, it also runs on Tuesdays from 11:00 to 12:00 and 14:30 to 16:30. Entry is €9.50. On certain weekdays, there's a lighter version called *Les Jardins Musicaux*, where only the music plays—no fountains—for €8.50.

Saturday nights in summer feature *Les Grandes Eaux Nocturnes*, a nighttime spectacle with illuminated groves, glowing pools, fountains set to music, and a fireworks finale. This takes place from early June to mid-September, from 20:30 to 23:00, with fireworks launching at 22:50. Entry for this evening show is €29.

Eating Options

Just inside the Château entrance, you'll find the Grand Café d'Orléans, which serves decent self-service meals perfect for a picnic in the gardens. Inside the grounds, there are snack bars and cafés, including one near the Latona Fountain. If you want more variety or something more sit-down, head into the town center of Versailles. Rue de Satory and Place du Marché have several good spots to eat.

Returning to Paris

To get back, walk about six minutes from the Château to the *Versailles Rive Gauche–Château* station. Any departing RER C train from that station goes back to Paris. If you're in a hurry or carrying a lot, a taxi back to the city center takes about 30 minutes and costs around €65, traffic permitting. There's also an option to take the metro-like yellow line (RER C), which makes 13 stops and drops you off at Saint-Michel–Notre-Dame.

Your Self-Guided Versailles Walk

This tour will guide you through the main areas of Versailles: the grand Château, the formal gardens, and the more intimate Trianon Palaces and Marie-Antoinette's Domaine, tucked away at the far end of the estate. Start by facing the large courtyard in front of the palace. The main entrance—labeled Entrance A—is easy to spot and usually has a queue forming.

The Château and Courtyard

Versailles began as a modest hunting lodge for the young Louis XIV. That original structure is still visible in the center of the palace, under the clock tower. His private bedroom, marked by three arched windows below the clock, faced east to catch the sunrise. The entire palace was laid out along an east-west axis to align with the sun. When Louis became king, he expanded the lodge into today's U-shaped layout, adding two long wings that cost about half of France's annual income at the time.

Imagine this courtyard 300 years ago: thousands of nobles would crowd in, dressed to impress and attended by their entourages. Sedan-chair taxis shuttled them between concerts and card games while servants raced around with platters of food. Carriages arrived from Paris, rolling past the gold gates with passengers in elaborate costumes. The crowd included everyone from courtiers and musicians to pickpockets and merchants.

How to Enter the Château

Once you pass through the entry gates, you'll find an information desk where you can grab a free map and check any bags. From there, re-enter the courtyard and follow the flow of visitors up into the palace. You'll walk through several rooms before arriving at the upper galleries. One of the first major stops is a space that opens up to the Royal Chapel.

Royal Chapel

Every day at 10:00 a.m., court musicians would begin to play, and the tall golden doors would swing open. Louis XIV and his family would enter the upper balcony to attend mass while the lower-ranking nobles stood below—backs to the altar—watching the king more than the priest. This chapel, while stunning, was something of a symbolic gesture. Versailles was designed to honor Louis himself as a divine ruler, and the chapel served as a nod to Christianity within an otherwise secular temple to the king's glory. This space also hosted major events, including the wedding of Marie-Antoinette to Louis XVI.

Hercules Drawing Room

This is where major balls, receptions, and state dinners were held. Picture a sea of wigs, powdered faces, and silk gowns swaying to live string music. Even the men wore rouge and beauty marks. Opposite the fireplace, you'll find a massive painting by Paolo Veronese showing the Marriage at Cana. Louis XIV loved this piece so much that he designed the entire room to match its columns, arches, and perspectives, making the painting feel like it blended seamlessly into the room. The ceiling is decorated with a dramatic image of Hercules flying through the clouds in his chariot, a visual tribute to one of Louis XIV's daughters, whose wedding was celebrated here.

From here, the path leads into the King's Wing, starting with a small green room. Look up—the ceiling features a soft pink goddess, a reminder that in Versailles, even the smallest spaces were designed to impress. The name of each room often comes from the ceiling painting above it, setting the tone for what follows.

Salon of Overflow

When the Hercules Room became too hot and crowded, guests would slip into this adjoining space to take a break. Coffee, liqueurs, chocolates and sometimes even light snacks like three-bean salad would circulate on silver trays. Louis XIV liked to entertain late into the night. If he took a gander and liked what he saw, he might invite you through a concealed door into his private study. There he would display prized items from his collection — including once the Mona Lisa, then in royal hands.

Venus Room

This room is all about love. It was meant to feel dreamy and lush, with painted columns reaching the space into imagined gardens in which Venus, goddess of deceit, lays her traps for the romantic. The scene from the Heaven column ceilings, which celebrates love and Louis himself, imagined as a Roman emperor surrounded by adoration. It started life as a lowly lodge before Louis turned it into his statement of power and pride — particularly after suffering the humiliations of the French parlements as a child. He made Versailles the archetypical comeback.

Diana Room

In this casual lounge, Louis shot billiards as courtiers reclined on Persian carpets. Music was drifting in from nearby salons. Louis was good at pool but hated losing — though, of course, no one was supposed to beat him. In the center is a bust of young Louis XIV by Bernini. Windswept curls and a confident, penetrating stare — peak image-building for a royal.

Above, the ceiling pays homage to Diana, goddess of the hunt — appropriate for Louis, who spent his days in pursuit, and his nights of courtly revelry.

It was more than just games, all this was strategy. Louis employed entertainment to keep nobles close and distracted. He ruled in isolation, filling his court with aristocrats who kept busy with cards and frivolity. The nobles often ended up in debt to the king—who was more than happy to lend them money and keep them in his pocket—in a common court game, similar to blackjack.

Mars Room

This was the guard room, formerly occupied by Louis's Swiss bodyguards. The ceiling features Mars, god of war, in a chariot drawn by wolves. It's a very masculine and bold space with these heavy red tones. Most of the furnishings here are not original, but they are of the period and do a good job of reconstructing the period.

Mercury Room

This room was Louis XIV's official bedroom, although he slept elsewhere.) But every morning, he was subjected to a ritual rising known as the lever du roi. Nobles congregated to see him rise, dress and pray — all meticulously staged to show off his piety and might. Everyone, even getting out of bed, was theatre at Versailles. You might see the king cracking his egg at breakfast or putting on his embroidered nightclothes before bed, guests could be treated to. And the bed, with its four-poster frame and rich fabrics, represented not just rest but monarchy itself.

Apollo Room

This was Louis XIV's official throne room, where he held court and received important guests. He sat on a raised platform under a ten-foot-high gold and silver canopy—nothing subtle here. The whole room shouts royal power. On the ceiling, the sun god Apollo (Louis' symbol) drives the chariot of the sun across the sky, warming even the Americas. Below, an Indian girl protects her eggs from a crocodile, a scene that somehow made sense at the time.

Above the fireplace hangs the famous portrait of Louis XIV by Hyacinthe Rigaud, painted when the king was 63. He's decked out in full regalia, with legs proudly shown off—a reminder that Louis was once a great dancer. At night, this room turned into a ballroom, with people dancing around the throne itself. Louis had more than 300 wigs and helped define fashion trends not only in France but across Europe and even in the American colonies. He styled himself as a kind of human god—Apollo in flesh and silk.

War Room

This chamber is a tribute to Louis' love of war, done in marble, gold, and painted drama. The ceiling shows the female figure of France hurling thunderbolts at her enemies. A sculpted relief shows Louis himself charging into battle on horseback, trampling his foes. Everything here is a reminder that Louis saw glory not just in peace and beauty but in conquest. But what showed off his power came next.

Hall of Mirrors

When this hall opened, it was a sensation. Mirrors were insanely expensive at the time, and here were 357 of them, stretched along a nearly 250-foot-long corridor. Each mirror arches across from a matching window that looks out over the royal gardens. Add twenty-four gold candelabras, eight busts of Roman emperors, and eight classical statues—and you've got a visual overload.

Try to picture this place lit by thousands of candles during a royal party. Nobles strutted in embroidered coats and powdered wigs, music echoed off the walls, and silver trays of hors d'oeuvres floated through the crowd. At one end sat the king, his throne moved here from the Apollo Room just for the event. These mirrors reflected a new attitude: self-image wasn't something to hide anymore—it was part of life's pleasures. People danced, drank, flirted, and soaked in the moment.

This space is the heart of Versailles—the grand design by Louis Le Vau, with interiors by Charles Le Brun, and those endless gardens by André Le Nôtre. It was also the site of a world-changing event: the signing of the Treaty of Versailles in 1919, which ended World War I but helped spark the next one.

Now, make your way to the end of the hall. The doors there lead to the Queen's quarters and the rest of the tour. Ready?

King's Chambers and Meeting Rooms

Enter the first of the King's private rooms—a grand space—and walk through it to arrive in Louis XIV's bedroom. The bed, with its balustrade and ornate drapery, is exactly where he slept and performed his morning "rising" ceremony for the court. Decorations changed with the seasons. This room isn't placed randomly—it's the precise center of the whole palace, opening onto the inner courtyard and facing east to catch the rising sun. It was built to be the symbolic heart of French royal power.

Now, picture the moment in 1789 when Louis XVI, a distant descendant of Louis XIV, stood at this very window. Crowds gathered below, demanding the end of the monarchy. The absolute power this room once symbolized was coming to an end.

Return to the Hall of Mirrors and walk to its far end, soaking in the view across the gardens as you go. From there, continue to the next section...

Peace Room

By the end of Louis XIV's reign, he was tired of war. This room tempers the battle themes of the War Room with images of reconciliation: Countries such as Germany, Holland and Spain are shown being compensated with peace. Cherubs romp among abandoned cannons, swords are being made into violins. The painting above the mantel depicts a young Louis XV extending an olive branch to Europe. It was a symbolic prayer for future peace — though history would take another turn.

Salon des Nobles

This pale green room is where the Queen and her court would have come together for conversation. They'd talk about politics, philosophy, the latest books, what was stylish, or what scandal was in circulation. The Enlightenment started in spaces like this — through talk, reading, inquiry of the old ways. These concepts led to the French Revolution.

Queen's Antechamber

It was here that the royal family ate in front of the public. Lunch might include four kinds of soup, filled birds, lamb, ham, fruit, pastry and a range of jams. The portrait of Marie-Antoinette here was meant to humanize her—there she is not a lavish queen but rather a concerned mother with her children.

Queen's Guard Room

On Oct. 5, 1789, enraged crowds descended on this area, furious over the shortage of food and royal excess. They stormed into this chamber and overcame the guards and then took the Queen and King away. The monarchy was broken. The palace was plundered, its majesty gutted. It sat empty for years before later leaders refurbished it as a national monument.

Coronation Room

Revolution gave way to empire. This room was redesigned under Napoleon, who crowned himself emperor here in 1804, reviving the imagery of Roman Caesars. In the large painting, you'll see him placing the crown on his head—refusing to let the Pope do it. By the window hangs a portrait of Napoleon in his early, youthful days, full of fire. Nearby, a later portrait shows him older, looking far more like the kind of monarch the revolution tried to overthrow.

This brings you to the end of the Château. Head downstairs and take a break at **Salon de Thé Angelina**, known for its pastries and hot chocolate. After that, continue further down and exit the palace. Turn right into **Les Jardins**, the vast gardens behind Versailles—ready for the next chapter of your walk.

Louis XIV believed he ruled by divine right—and he made sure Versailles reflected that. The gardens aren't just pretty landscaping; they're a physical symbol of total control. Every hedge, path, and fountain was designed to show the king's dominance over nature itself.

The gardens are massive. For many, a short walk around the trimmed hedges near the palace is enough. But even if you don't plan to head to the Trianon or the Queen's Hamlet, a walk down to the Apollo Basin is worth it. It takes about ten minutes one way, and the views are some of the best in Versailles.

Start by entering the gardens and heading to the top of the staircase that looks down over the entire grounds. From this high point, turn your back to the palace...

The View Down

This is one of the most striking views in Versailles. There's no fence, no visual end—just an endless stretch of geometry and symmetry. The entire estate lines up along an eight-mile axis, from the palace to the far end of the town. This was one of Europe's earliest examples of large-scale urban planning, inspiring places like Washington, D.C., and Brasília.

Look straight ahead. In the center is the Apollo Fountain, and beyond that, the Grand Canal. On either side of the long Royal Drive are groves—mini gardens lined with trees brought in from all over France, shaped and planted in perfect geometric form. Statues and fountains were scattered throughout. Out of the original 1,500 fountains, about 300 remain.

Now, walk down the steps toward the Apollo Fountain. Halfway there, you'll come to...

Latona Basin

This round fountain tells a myth. At the top, you'll see statues of the young Apollo and Diana, with their mother Latona facing the direction of the Apollo Fountain. The story goes that after Zeus got Latona pregnant, she was insulted by locals. As revenge, the gods turned those villagers into frogs and lizards. You'll spot them among the sculptures.

From here, keep walking toward the Apollo Fountain. If you have time and energy, take a detour into the woods on the left side of the Royal Drive. Hidden among the trees is the **Colonnade**, a circular marble structure with sculptures, water, and shade—perfect for a quiet moment away from the crowds.

Navigating the Gardens

By Foot: Going to the château, and you must walk to the Grand Canal and continue to the Petit Trianon, the Grand Trianon, and finally, the Domaine de Marie-Antoinette. The walk takes 45 to 60 minutes, including stops for sightseeing. It's a pleasant route, especially if the weather is good.

On Bike: Bikes are available for rent by the Grand Canal—€9 per hour or €20 for a half day. Open daily from 10 a.m. to 6 p.m. Bikes are not allowed inside the Trianon or Domaine areas, but you can park them nearby and continue on foot.

Or by Train: This slow-moving tram starts just behind the château. It follows a loop around the gardens, stopping at the Grand Canal, Petit Trianon, and Grand Trianon. It costs €8.50 round-trip or €4.60 one-way. Runs every 15–30 minutes, Tuesday to

Sunday from 11:30 to 19:00, and on Mondays from 11:00 to 17:00 (shorter hours in winter). You can't hop on and off at will—it's one loop per ticket.

And unusually a Golf Cart: A fun option if you're short on time or energy. Golf carts can be rented for €38 per hour (plus €9 per additional 15 minutes) for up to four people. They follow a fixed path and are not allowed in the Trianon or Domaine areas. Rentals are located behind the château, near the canal entrance.

Colonnade

Instead of admiring Roman ruins, Louis XIV had some made. Holding up white stone arches are 64 red marble columns in this elegant circular structure. The colonnade, 100 feet wide, was a favored venue for aristocratic picnics, with live classical music. It resembles a theatrical backdrop designed to mimic the splendor of ancient Rome.

Apollo Basin

This is the centerpiece of Versailles' grand fountains. And in the center, Apollo, god of the sun, on his rising chariot, pulled by sea horses, half-submerged as if emergent from the mist. When the fountains are going, the whole thing comes alive, suggesting sunrise itself.

The water system at Versailles was an engineering marvel — gravity-fed fountains that were supplied water pumped from the Seine. Many of these subterranean pipes are in use to this day.

From here, turn around and look back at the palace. You will know how far you have come — and how much of the estate still is in front of you.

Grand Canal

The Grand Canal, a mile long, used to be navigated like little Venice. Royal visitors could ride in gondolas while musicians entertained from boats alongside. It was Louis XIV's idea of luxury leisure. Today, it's a nice place to unwind, rent a rowboat or simply take in the views.

Next up: the Trianon Palaces and Domaine de Marie-Antoinette, a quieter, more intimate side of Versailles that lies tucked away toward the back of the gardens. You require a ticket to go within but it's worth it. Tell me if you'd like to see the next section rewritten, as well.

The Trianon Palaces and Queen's Gardens

Originally Versailles was meant to provide the king a respite from court in Paris. But gradually it became just as frenzied and political. So Louis XIV erected a smaller, quieter palace nearby — the Grand Trianon. Later Marie Antoinette built a more private getaway: an estate in the country, with gardens, ponds and a quaint hamlet that seemed far from the business of royalty.

The Grand Trianon

Nestled amid graceful gardens and rose-pink stone, the Grand Trianon was the king's hideaway. Louis XIV typically spent several nights a week here, relishing peace outside the heart of the palace. The rooms inside are furnished with a hodgepodge of furniture and decor from various rulers — Louis XIV, Napolcon, and then some.

The Salon des Glaces (Room 2) is one highlight, a lustrous hall where mirrors dating to Louis XIV sit next to Empire furniture from Napoleon. Immediately adjacent is Room 3, the bedroom of Empress Maria Feodorovna. Imagine waking up and opening the curtains to view the manicured, symmetrical gardens.

Outside, a long, columned walkway, called the Peristyle, connects the building's two wings. It used to have glass windows, so it could be enjoyed even if the weather wasn't cooperating.

This room has seen many transformations—it was a theater during Louis XIV's reign, a gaming room under Louis XV, and later became a family parlor for Napoleon. After his fall, King Louis-Philippe turned the palace into his official royal residence.

Do be sure to pop into Room 11, the Malachite Room. It's decorated with vibrant green malachite vases, basins and candleholders — presents from Russian Czar Alexander I to Napoleon.

Complete the loop around the Grand Trianon, then follow signs toward the French Pavilion. Take a footbridge to reach it.

French Pavilion

This diminutive, cream-colored structure is generally off-limits to visitors, but it's not hard to admire from the street. Its layout features big French windows that swing open to invite in the evening air. Marie Antoinette frequently entertained close friends here for music, games and quiet time in the garden.

From here, start walking toward the Petit Trianon, a nearly square building on your right. Hall, pit stop pues take a quick flickeren at...

Marie-Antoinette's Theater

This little 100-seat theater was one of Marie-Antoinette's favorite places. She and friends put on plays here, sometimes with the queen herself in the cast. Those blue-and-gold interiors, velvet curtains and miniature stage are all royal dollhouse. Built for fun though it is, it is a quiet manifestation of her desire to escape the pressures of royal life.

Belvedere, Rock, and Grotto

A short walk from the theater leads to the Pavilion at the Belvedere, an elegant octagonal structure more glass than wood. It used to be where music was played and summer parties held. To the left, the Rock is a manmade slope with waterfalls that cascade into a pond. The Grotto, a secluded cave-like area for quiet reflection, is on the right.

Keep walking east past the Belvedere and cross over a small stream. Soon you will spot a round stone tower and a few ramshackle houses. This is the entrance to...

The Hamlet

Marie-Antoinette dreamed of peace, of a rural life — not the real, hard life of peasant farmers, but a stylized version populated by gardens, animals and quiet charm. She created this Hamlet, with cottages, a working dairy, a mill, a pigeon house and pens for animals. A wooden bridge connects the main house with two buildings that contain a billiard room, library, dining room and sitting rooms. Servants tended goats, cows, chickens and ducks nearby, so it was a real farm, just made fancy for royalty.

Petit Trianon

The Petit Trianon was built for Madame de Pompadour by Louis XV. It later went to Countess du Barry and then to Marie-Antoinette, who made it her refuge. The palace's clean lines and small scale provided her space to flee court pressure. She placed a merry-go-round on the lawn and planted flower beds.

Inside, you'll find portraits, furniture and even her private bathroom — fitted with an endearingly modern wooden-plank toilet. Far from the image that prevailed in public, Marie-Antoinette was a young woman from Vienna who never really found her footing amid palace politics. The Petit Trianon was her sanctuary, a miniature universe separate from Versailles and the revolution brewing beyond its gates.

Returning to the Château

It's about a 30-minute walk back to the main palace from the Petit Trianon. If heading directly to the train station, tack on another 10 minutes. Or, return by Petit Train — there's a stop at the end of the Petit Trianon walls.

If you're employing the Versailles map from earlier in this guide, you'll be able to take a somewhat shorter road through the village to get back to the station.

This concludes your visit to Versailles. Once here, you can return to Paris, where world-class museums, iconic landmarks, historic churches and vibrant neighborhoods beckon.

In the rest of this guide, we've divided the city into manageable walking routes, with tips on how to save time, skip lines and find good places to eat nearby. With the grandeur of Versailles behind you, Paris awaits.

Tickets and Passes

In Paris, purchasing tickets ahead of time isn't merely helpful — often, it's essential. Most highly rated attractions require timed-entry reservations, and even sights that don't can have very long lines, particularly during high season (April to October) and on weekends. If you don't want to spend hours waiting in line, it's advisable to plan ahead and purchase tickets online.

The Louvre, Musée de l'Orangerie, Sainte-Chapelle and Versailles need advance reservations. You can't enter these places without a time slot. For other popular sites, like the Eiffel Tower, Catacombs and Conciergerie, reservations aren't required, but highly recommended. These sites tend to sell out multiple days ahead, particularly in summer or school holidays.

When you book ahead, you're not skipping security — you still go through screening, much like you would in an airport. But you will save some time because you will skip the ticket counter — which can easily take 30–60 minutes or more. It's a straightforward way to help your visit go more smoothly and be less stressful. Also bring a reusable water bottle — access to water isn't always easy, and you should stay hydrated, especially in warm weather.

Tickets can be booked online via each site's official website. Save third-party resellers for when you absolutely have to. The official sites may require you to set up an account and navigate a few steps, but don't be deterred — it will save you in extra fees or hidden markups.

After purchasing a ticket, you typically get a confirmation via email that includes a QR code. Add the email to their phone, or download the PDF. You don't need to print it, but make sure your phone is charged. At the entrance, follow the line that says "Billet réservé" or "Visitors with reservation."

A museum pass for Paris is also not enough to amuse someone and they will still be required to reserve a time slot before visiting an attraction like the Louvre. Reservations are free, but need to be made in advance. On the booking site, choose the option for "Paris Museum Pass holders" or "Gratuit" (free) and input your pass number. A confirmation email with your timed ticket will be sent to you.

What the Paris Museum Pass Includes

The **Paris Museum Pass** gives you entry to more than 50 museums and monuments around the city and suburbs. This includes major sites like the **Louvre, Orsay Museum, Sainte-Chapelle, Rodin Museum, Pantheon, Versailles**, and **Arc de Triomphe**. It's a great option if you plan to visit multiple museums in a short time and want to skip general admission lines.

The pass comes in three durations:

- **2 consecutive days**: €52

- **4 consecutive days**: €66

- **6 consecutive days**: €78

There are **no discounts** for seniors or youth, but children under 18 (or EU residents under 26) often get free entry anyway, so the pass may not be necessary for them. To get the most value, plan to visit at least two or three major sights each day the pass is active.

Sites **not covered** by the Paris Museum Pass include:

- The **Eiffel Tower**

- The **Catacombs**

- **Montparnasse Tower**

- **Opéra Garnier** (except for the self-guided visit, sometimes included)

- **Marmottan Monet Museum**

It's best to check the official list online before you buy the pass.

Where to Buy the Pass

You can buy the Paris Museum Pass online (and pick it up in Paris) or in person at tourist offices, major museums, and selected gift shops near major sights. However, avoid getting it at big places like the **Louvre** or **Orsay**, where lines may be long or stock may run out. The Museum Pass is also available at FNAC stores and at the **La Civette du Carrousel** newsstand under the Louvre (cash only).

Only activate the pass on the first day you're ready to use it, and plan accordingly. Museums tend to be closed one day a week—most often **Monday or Tuesday**—so make sure you're not activating it when several top museums are closed.

If Tickets Are Sold Out Online

If your preferred time slot is fully booked on the official site, your options aren't gone. Try a **third-party seller** offering "coupe-file" (skip-the-line) tickets. These often cost more but can be worth it for convenience. Reputable third-party options include:

- FNAC (a chain of department stores)

- Paris tourist offices

- Tour companies like **Paris Webservices** or **Fat Tire Tours**

These may bundle the ticket with a short guided visit or audio guide to justify the markup.

In short: always try to book early—at least a week ahead, if possible. For high-season visits, even sooner is better. This will help you avoid queues, secure good times for visits, and save energy for enjoying the actual sights.

HISTORIC CENTER OF PARIS

Sainte-Chapelle

Tucked inside the former royal palace, Sainte-Chapelle is a Gothic gem that dazzles with its 1,100 square feet of stained-glass windows. The upper chapel glows with scenes from the Bible depicted in luminous reds, blues, and purples—especially stunning on a sunny day. Originally built to house Christian relics, it now draws visitors who come just to stand in awe of the kaleidoscopic light. Entry is by timed ticket; included in Museum Pass. Booking online is strongly recommended, as space is limited.

Notre-Dame Cathedral

Standing for over 850 years, Notre-Dame is the heart of Paris—both spiritually and geographically. The cathedral was badly damaged by a fire in 2019 that destroyed its roof and spire. Restoration is underway, and although the interior remains closed for now, the newly rebuilt spire and facade can be admired up close. The plaza in front is open again, and you can walk around the perimeter to view the sculpted details and iconic flying buttresses. Don't miss "Point Zéro" in front of the cathedral—the bronze marker from which all distances in France are measured. For more historical context, see the "Historical Walks" chapter.

Riverside Promenades and Paris Plages

Both banks of the Seine offer scenic, car-free paths ideal for walking, biking, or just relaxing. On the Left Bank, the promenade stretches past the Eiffel Tower and Orsay Museum. On the Right Bank, another route runs from the Louvre to the Bastille, lined with cafés and wide open spaces. In summer, the Right Bank transforms into Paris Plages—a temporary beach setup complete with lounge chairs, food stands, and pop-up sports activities. Locals and tourists alike gather here to unwind by the river.

Conciergerie

This former royal palace turned prison became infamous during the French Revolution. Marie-Antoinette was held here before being sent to the guillotine. Today, you can visit her reconstructed cell and walk through stark stone halls lined with the names of those who were executed. Exhibits in English cover the building's transformation and the lives of its prisoners.

€11.50 for timed entry; €18.50 for a combo ticket with Sainte-Chapelle. Included in the Museum Pass. Open daily 9:30–18:00. Multimedia guide €5.

2 Boulevard du Palais, Métro: Cité +33 1 53 40 60 80

Paris Archaeological Crypt (Crypte Archéologique)

Beneath the plaza in front of Notre Dame lies a fascinating underground museum that reveals the layered history of the city. Here, you can walk past remnants of Roman baths, a medieval street, an ancient wall, and a Roman building with remnants of a heating system. Multimedia panels guide you through the shifting centuries of Paris's urban development.

€8 admission, included in the Museum Pass. Open Tuesday–Sunday, 10:00–18:00. Closed Mondays. The audioguide €5. The entry is located just in front of the cathedral. +33 1 55 42 50 10

Paris Museum Quarter

Louvre Museum

The Louvre is not just Europe's oldest and largest museum — it is also one of its most iconic. Once a royal palace, it became a public museum after the French Revolution and now contains more than 30,000 works of art in a space of 650,000 square feet. The Louvre's encyclopedic collection covers ancient cultures through 19th-century France.

Its most famous attractions include the Mona Lisa, the Venus de Milo and the Winged Victory of Samothrace, but it is also loaded with Egyptian artifacts, Greek sculptures, Renaissance masterpieces and French neoclassical works. To navigate effectively, pick a theme or time period. Italian paintings and large French historical canvases do best in the Denon Wing. The Sully Wing includes antiquities, like Greek and Roman artifacts, and the Richelieu Wing features sculptures, tapestries and Napoleon III's opulent apartments.

Reservations are required.

Tickets cost €17, free with a Museum Pass (but still need a timed-entry reservation).

Open Wed–Mon 9:00–18:00 (Tue closed); Fri until 21:45.

Métro: Palais Royal–Musée du Louvre. www.louvre.fr

Rodin Museum (Musée Rodin)

Located in a charming 18th-century mansion and a serene sculpture garden, this museum is dedicated to Auguste Rodin, France's greatest sculptor. Iconic pieces such as The Thinker, The Kiss and The Gates of Hell are on display here, showcasing Rodin's innate emotional power and rare ability to convey movement in stone and bronze. Many works seem almost unfinished by design, confronting raw material as if they were creatures emerging from the dark. You can track Rodin's process inside the museum — from clay studies to polished bronzes — and read about his passionate and tormented affair with fellow sculptor Camille Claudel. The garden has many large sculptures, flower beds and benches for reflection. It's among Paris's most tranquil art spaces.

Admission: €13; combo with Orsay Museum €24; free on first Sunday of month (Oct–March). Included in Museum Pass.

Open Tuesday–Sun from 10:00–18:30. Closed Mon.

Gardens close at dusk Oct–March. Audio guide: €6.

77 Rue de Varenne. Métro: Varenne.

+33 1 44 18 61 10.

Army Museum & Napoleon's Tomb (Musée de l'Armée / Les Invalides)

Located in a 17th-century veterans' hospital commissioned by Louis XIV, it's one of the premier military museums in Europe. The centerpiece is Napoleon Bonaparte's tomb, housed in a massive red porphyry coffin placed under the gold-dome, church. The museum itself is a survey of the entire arc of French military history — from early armor and medieval swords to WWI trench warfare and WWII resistance efforts.

Here you will find exhibits about France's role in the world wars, including propaganda posters, maps, uniforms and audio recordings. Charles de Gaulle, commander of the

Free French Forces in World War II who played such a role in modernizing France, gets his own section.

Admission: €14, covered by Museum Pass.

Open daily 10:00–18:00; Tomb open late until 21:00 on Tue.

Multimedia guide: €5.

129 Rue de Grenelle. Métro: La Tour-Maubourg, Varenne, or Invalides.

+33 1 44 42 38 77

Orangerie Museum (Musée de l'Orangerie)

Small and understated, this museum in a corner of the Tuileries Gardens is a hidden gem. The star of the show: Claude Monet's Water Lilies — eight gigantic curved murals that fill two oval rooms, conceived as an immersive meditation on nature. Monet created them late in life, in his garden at Giverny, when he was losing his sight. Downstairs is the Jean Walter and Paul Guillaume collection, with key works of late Impressionist and early modernist periods. Seek out portraits and colorful still lifes by Modigliani, Renoir, Matisse, Cézanne, Utrillo and Picasso.

Admission: €12.50; combo with Orsay €18; included in Museum Pass. Free on the first Sunday of each month.

Open Wed–Mon, 9:00–18:00 (last entry 17:15). Closed Tue.

Audioguide: €5; Guided tours: €6.

Located inside the Tuileries Garden near Place de la Concorde. Métro: Concorde.

+33 1 44 77 80 07 — www.musee-orangerie.fr

Eiffel Tower and Nearby Attractions

Eiffel Tower

This 1,063-foot-tall structure, built for the World's Fair in 1889, was once considered an eyesore. Today, it's the iconic image of Paris. Though many other towers now hold greater height, few towers are as magical to stand under or atop as the Eiffel Tower.

Visitors may take elevators or ascend stairs to three separate viewing tiers, each one providing sweeping vistas of the city and beyond. The upper level, almost 900 feet above, is windy but unforgettable. You can see all the big landmarks from here — Notre-Dame, the Arc de Triomphe, the Seine, even a little Statue of Liberty far west on the river.

Reservations are highly recommended, particularly in the peak season. Open daily with extended summer hours. Refer to the Eiffel Tower section for practical details on how to get and time tickets, as well as how to appreciate the tower and surrounding areas best.

Rue Cler

A few blocks from the Eiffel Tower, Rue Cler is one of Paris's most charming pedestrian streets. It's lined with family-run shops selling cheese, wine, bread, chocolates, and fresh produce. Locals shop here daily, and it's a perfect place to pick up picnic supplies before heading to Champ de Mars or the riverbanks.

Marmottan Museum

This lesser-known gem is home to the world's largest collection of Claude Monet, including works dating to the late 19th century. This is where you'll find *Impression, Sunrise*—the iconic painting that gave the Impressionist movement its name. You'll also find beautiful large water-lily canvases and works by Berthe Morisot, alongside pieces by Renoir, Degas and others.

This museum, which occupies a stately private home in the 16th arrondissement, is one of the quieter ones. If you're a Monet fan, or looking for a respite from the crowds, it's a trip worth making.

€12 admission (not included in Museum Pass). Closed Mondays.

2 Rue Louis-Boilly, Métro: La Muette. www.marmottan.fr

Deportation Memorial

Hidden behind Notre-Dame at the far tip of Île de la Cité, this underground memorial honors the 200,000 French victims of Nazi concentration camps. Its narrow corridors, low ceilings, and flickering light create a powerful sense of isolation and loss. A sobering and moving experience.

Paris Sewer Museum (Musée des Égouts de Paris)

This unusual and slightly smelly tour takes you through a real section of the city's functioning sewer system. You'll learn how Paris evolved from tossing waste into the Seine to building an advanced 1,500-mile network. Displays cover engineering, water flow, sanitation, and even pop culture (like Les Misérables). €9, covered by Museum Pass. Located beneath Pont de l'Alma on the Left Bank, near the Eiffel Tower. Closed Mondays.

Best Views in Paris

Eiffel Tower – Paris from above, the ultimate viewpoint.

Place du Trocadéro – The classic spot to take photos of the tower, especially at night.

Arc de Triomphe – See the starburst of avenues and the Champs-Élysées, especially striking at sunset.

Sacré-Cœur Steps – Perched atop Montmartre, enjoy both the view and the lively square.

Galeries Lafayette Rooftop – Free and central with a close view of the Opera and beyond.

Montparnasse Tower – The only modern skyscraper in central Paris; fantastic panoramic views.

Centre Pompidou – Combine great views with modern art.

Paris Ferris Wheel (when operating) – A temporary but fun perspective.

Windo Skybar at Hyatt Regency – A drink with a view from the 34th floor; panoramic and peaceful.

Left Bank

Cluny Museum (Musée National du Moyen Âge)

This outstanding museum of the Middle Ages is set in a fabulous building — part Roman bathhouse, part Gothic mansion. It has a beautiful collection of stained glass, metalwork, statues, altar pieces and tapestries from medieval France. The highlight is the renowned Lady and the Unicorn series. The six great tapestries full of symbolism represent the five senses and a hazy sixth sense often described as either "desire" or "understanding."

Each tapestry depicts a noblewoman, a lion, and a unicorn in different scenes. The sixth piece, À Mon Seul Désir, is much interpreted — what is the woman reaching toward or relinquishing? The tapestries are displayed in a dark and quiet gallery to preserve the fragile fabrics.

Admission is €12 (Museum Pass includes); free first Sunday of month. (October to April: Open Tuesday–Sunday, 9:30–18:15; last entry 45 minutes before closing.

Closed Mondays. Located at 6 Place Paul Painlevé, near Métro stops Cluny-La Sorbonne, St-Michel, or Odéon. +33 1 53 73 78 10.

Latin Quarter (Quartier Latin)

Just across the river from Notre Dame, this historic neighborhood once formed the core of Roman Paris. It gets its name from the Latin language, spoken by students at the Sorbonne during medieval times. Today, it's known for its mix of student life, cafés, bookshops, and lively streets. Writers, poets, and philosophers used to gather in its cafés and salons—Jean-Paul Sartre, Simone de Beauvoir, and Ernest Hemingway all spent time here.

Today, the charm remains. Wander its narrow alleys and find a mix of tourist shops, cheap eats, jazz clubs, and bakeries. Despite the crowds, it still holds a creative and bohemian spirit.

Luxembourg Garden (Jardin du Luxembourg)

This is one of the green spaces that locals love best in Paris. The 60-acre garden, which was created in the 1600s for Queen Marie de Medici, has shady alleys, flowerbeds, fountains and open lawns. Local people flock here to read, sunbathe, play chess, jog or take children to the playground or puppet theater.

The palace's octagonal pond is a highlight — children rent mini sailboats to paddle around with sticks. The adjacent chairs lend themselves to lounging and people-watching. The French Senate convenes inside the palace, but the grounds are open to all.

Open daily from early morning until dusk. Closest Métro: Odéon; RER B: Luxembourg station.

Catacombs of Paris (Les Catacombes)

Beneath the Left Bank lies a network of former limestone quarries that became a massive underground ossuary in the late 18th century. The remains of around six million Parisians were moved here when overcrowded cemeteries posed health risks.

You'll walk about a mile through eerie tunnels lined with carefully arranged bones and skulls, many forming patterns and walls up to five feet high. A sign at the entrance reads: *"Stop! This is the empire of the dead."*

It's a sobering but fascinating experience. Book timed-entry tickets in advance—€29 includes an audio guide.

Not included in the Museum Pass. Same-day €15 tickets are sometimes available.

Open Tuesday–Sunday, 10:00–20:30. Last entry one hour before closing. Located at 1 Place Denfert-Rochereau, Métro: Denfert-Rochereau. +33 1 43 22 47 63.

St. Sulpice Church

This massive church, often overshadowed by Notre Dame, is one of Paris's hidden gems. Its front towers and neoclassical façade resemble London's St. Paul's Cathedral. Inside, you'll find Delacroix murals, a monument to Joan of Arc, and an impressive pipe organ—considered one of the best in the world.

If you love organ music, visit on Sunday: a mini concert is played after the 11:00 Mass by the resident organist, Daniel Roth. The acoustics and instruments together create a memorable experience.

Free to enter. Open daily 7:30–19:30. Closest Métro: St-Sulpice or Mabillon.

Panthéon

Originally built in the 18th century as a church and converted into a civic monument, the Panthéon honors great French figures — Voltaire, Rousseau, Victor Hugo, Marie Curie, among others, are buried in the crypt. The neoclassical design, inspired by Rome's Pantheon, features a grand dome and Corinthian columns. Within is Foucault's Pendulum, a pendulous device that demonstrated Earth's rotation.

For some of the best bang-for-your-buck views in Paris, climb to the dome (extra €3.50).

Admission: €11.50, included in Museum Pass; dome access not included. Open daily 10:00–18:30 (until 18:00 in winter); last entry 45 minutes before closing. Closest Métro: Cardinal Lemoine. +33 1 44 32 18 00.

Montparnasse Tower (Tour Montparnasse)

Often criticized for its plain appearance, this 60-story tower is one of the only skyscrapers in central Paris. But what it lacks in charm, it makes up for in the views. From the 56th-floor indoor deck and the open-air rooftop, you'll see all of Paris including the Eiffel Tower from a perfect distance.

It's rarely crowded, and sunset is a great time to visit. A café and photo displays are available on the observation deck. Not covered by the Museum Pass. Entry costs about €18, with discounts for children and some two-person combos.

Open daily: Oct–March 10:00–22:30, April–Sept 9:30–23:30.

Entrance is on Rue de l'Arrivée; from the Métro, follow signs to Exit 1. +33 1 45 38 52 56.

Champs-Élysées and Surroundings

Champs-Élysées

Often called the backbone of Paris, the Champs-Élysées is one of the city's most iconic avenues—buzzing with traffic and activity most days, except for the first Sunday of each month when it's delightfully car-free. Despite its global fame, the boulevard has managed to hold on to its Parisian character, and a walk along its nearly two-mile stretch remains an essential experience.

Originally laid out by Louis XIV in 1667, the avenue quickly became a fashionable playground for aristocrats parading their carriages. By the 1920s, it symbolized Parisian luxury, lined with grand mansions, upscale hotels, and refined restaurants. Today, that historic opulence blends with modern commercial life—flagship boutiques, bustling cafés, and popular hangouts for both celebrities and locals alike.

Start your stroll at the Arc de Triomphe and head down the northern side of the avenue. At No. 116, you'll spot the famous Lido, home to Paris's largest burlesque cabaret and a multiplex cinema. Directly across the street stands the Louis Vuitton flagship store (No. 101), an unmistakable symbol of French fashion. A little farther down is the legendary Fouquet's café (No. 99), beloved by French film stars whose names you'll find etched into the pavement outside—though the coffee prices inside might make you pause.

For a more budget-friendly treat, stop at Ladurée (No. 75) for a takeaway macaron and a dash of old-world charm. As you continue, you'll pass international names like Sephora, Disney, and Renault, leading you to the busy Rond-Point (Métro: Franklin D. Roosevelt). From there, you can either end your walk or carry on toward Place de la Concorde, crowned by its towering Egyptian obelisk.

Arc de Triomphe

Commissioned by Napoleon to honor his 1805 victory at Austerlitz, the Arc de Triomphe has since become a symbol of both triumph and remembrance. It has marked key moments in French history—from Napoleon's own funeral procession to the German occupation during World War II, and the jubilant return of Charles de Gaulle after the country's liberation. Take your time exploring the arch's elaborate sculptures, including a proud Napoleon and a fierce Lady Liberty, among other powerful reliefs. Beneath the arch lies the Tomb of the Unknown Soldier, where a flame is solemnly rekindled every evening at 6:30 p.m.

Climb the 284 steps to the rooftop viewing platform and you'll be rewarded with panoramic views stretching across Paris. From this height, even the chaotic traffic below takes on a certain beauty. The Arc sits at the heart of the Axe Historique—a grand axis that stretches from the Louvre to the modern Grande Arche at La Défense. Look down and you'll see 12 avenues converging in a star-shaped pattern (étoile), forming one of the city's most iconic roundabouts. In a rare twist of traffic law, cars entering the circle have the right of way, meaning those already inside must yield.

Admission is €13 and includes rooftop access. Entry is free on the first Sunday of the month from November to March and is covered by the Museum Pass. Tickets are timed and can be booked online. The monument is open daily from 10 a.m. to 11 p.m. (until 10:30 p.m. October through March), with last entry 45 minutes before closing. To reach it safely, use the underground pedestrian passage at Place Charles de Gaulle. Métro: Charles de Gaulle–Étoile. Info: +33 1 55 37 73 77.

Paris Ferris Wheel (Roue de Paris)

Situated on the north side of the Tuileries Garden, the Paris Ferris Wheel (Roue de Paris) is a giant wheel that provides stunning panoramic views of the city's most recognizable monuments, including the Louvre and the Eiffel Tower. Part of a vibrant summer funfair, it's nestled among colorful rides, classic carnival games and snack stands, creating a festive experience that's perfect for families, couples and visitors of all ages. Tickets are €12 per person, and cover two slow, scenic revolutions that give you time to take in the sights. Two passengers will fit comfortably in each gondola. Open daily from late June to late August, the Ferris wheel is an ideal stop during a summer night out.

Petit Palais (and Musée des Beaux-Arts)

Step inside to discover a rich array of artwork spanning centuries. The ground floor showcases an impressive selection of paintings and sculptures from the 1600s to the 1800s. Downstairs, the galleries take you on a journey from ancient Greek artifacts all the way to the elegance of the Art Nouveau period. Among the standout pieces are Courbet's provocative The Sleepers (1866), Monet's luminous Sunset on the Seine at Lavacourt (1880), and works by Mary Cassatt and other renowned Impressionists.

Admission is free. The museum is open Tuesday through Sunday from 10 a.m. to 6 p.m., with extended hours on Friday evenings during special exhibitions. Closed Mondays. You'll find it just across from the Grand Palais, on Avenue Winston Churchill. Métro: Champs-Élysées–Clemenceau. Phone: +33 1 53 43 40 00.

Opéra and Surroundings

Opéra Garnier

This opulent belle époque theater, completed in 1875 for Napoleon III, is one of the most iconic buildings in Paris. Standing at the **Opéra Métro** stop, you'll get a postcard view of the façade, complete with Corinthian columns, golden statues, and ornate carvings. Beneath it lies a hidden underground lake that inspired *The Phantom of the Opera*.

Inside, you're in for a visual feast: a sweeping **Grand Staircase**, gilded mirrors, chandeliers, red velvet seating, and the spectacular performance hall with its massive **seven-ton chandelier** and **ceiling painted by Marc Chagall**. Guided tours, audio tours, and self-guided walks are available, or you can attend a ballet or opera performance to see it come to life.

Also nearby are the historic **Café de la Paix**, **Galeries Lafayette** (with its rooftop terrace), and the **Fragonard Perfume Museum**, which are all worth stopping into before or after your visit.

Tickets: €14 for general entry; reduced to €4 if you've visited the Orsay Museum within the past 8 days. Not covered by the Museum Pass. Open daily 10:00–16:15 (until 17:15 mid-July through August). English guided tours are usually daily at 14:00 (book online); arrive early for security checks.

Address: 8 Rue Scribe. Métro: Opéra. RER A: Auber. Check the box office or website for performance schedules (box office open Mon–Sat 11:30–18:30 and one hour before curtain, closed Sun).

Jacquemart-André Museum

This elegant mansion gives you a rare look into how the wealthy lived in 19th-century Paris. Art-collecting couple Edouard André and Nélie Jacquemart filled their home with masterpieces by **Rembrandt**, **Fragonard**, **Botticelli**, **Bellini**, and **Uccello**, displayed throughout salons, staircases, and a private chapel.

The museum is not huge, but it's peaceful and filled with atmosphere. The on-site **tearoom** is popular for its cakes, quiche, and refined vibe, often considered one of the loveliest café spots in Paris. From here, you can walk north along **Rue de Courcelles** to reach **Parc Monceau**, a beautifully landscaped park with classical statues and romantic corners.

Tickets: €12, with special exhibit surcharges of €3–5. Not covered by a Museum Pass. Open daily 10:00–18:00; Mondays until 20:30 during special exhibits. Buy online in advance (there's a €2 fee).

Address: 158 Boulevard Haussmann. Métro: St-Philippe-du-Roule. Tel: +33 1 45 62 11 59.

Fragonard Perfume Museum

Just a block from the opera house, this museum offers a short and free tour through the history of perfume-making. You'll see antique distillation equipment, early fragrance bottles and learn how perfumes were crafted in the 18th and 19th centuries. Afterward, you can sample scents and purchase perfumes in the shop, many of which are made using traditional techniques in the Fragonard factory.

Entrance is free. Open daily 9:00–18:00, no need to book in advance.

Address: 3-5 Square de l'Opéra-Louis Jouvet. Métro: Opéra.

Galeries Lafayette Rooftop and Dome

Even if you're not in the mood to shop, Galeries Lafayette is worth a stop. Inside, look up to see the stunning **Art Nouveau stained-glass dome**, and take the escalators to the rooftop terrace, which offers one of the best **free views of Paris**. From here, you can see the Eiffel Tower, Montmartre, and the Opéra Garnier itself. The rooftop is quiet compared to the nearby tourist spots and is a perfect place for a break.

Free to enter. Rooftop open during store hours: Mon–Sat 10:00–20:00 (until 20:30 during holidays).

Address: 40 Boulevard Haussmann. Métro: Chaussée d'Antin–La Fayette or Opéra.

The Marais Area

Carnavalet Museum (Musée Carnavalet)

Housed in two beautiful mansions in the heart of the Marais, the Carnavalet Museum tells the story of Paris from ancient times to the present. It's well-organized, with English signage and summaries in most rooms. The museum's highlight is the immersive section on the **French Revolution**, featuring personal items, political cartoons, royal memorabilia, and chilling relics from the Reign of Terror—including a lock of Marie-Antoinette's hair and a guillotine blade.

The top floor walks you through the transformation of Paris in the **19th and 20th centuries**, starting with **Baron Haussmann's** massive urban redesign, the rise of **art nouveau**, and scenes from the **belle époque**, including cabarets, the Eiffel Tower, and early aviation. There's also a modern wing with exhibits covering **WWI, WWII, the May '68 protests**, and the evolution of today's Paris.

The museum is ideal for those who want to understand how Paris grew into the city we know now.

Admission is free. Open Tuesday–Sun, 10:00–18:00; closed Monday.

Address: 16 Rue des Francs-Bourgeois. Métro: St-Paul.

Montmartre and Sacré-Cœur

Atop Paris' only real hill sits **Sacré-Cœur Basilica**, with its white domes visible from much of the city. It may look ancient, but it was completed only in 1914. The interior glows with gold mosaics, most notably one of Christ's hearts burning with love for humanity. You'll also find statues, a crypt, and stained glass honoring **Joan of Arc**. For a panoramic view, climb the **300-step spiral staircase** to the dome—worth the effort on a clear day.

Behind the basilica, wander into **Place du Tertre**, once a haunt for artists like Toulouse-Lautrec, Modigliani, and Utrillo. Now, it's crowded with tourists, street artists, and overpriced cafés, but there's still charm in the cobblestone streets and the memory of its bohemian past.

Stop by the **Montmartre Museum**, housed in the oldest building on the hill. It showcases paintings, vintage posters, photos, and video clips tracing Montmartre's artistic legacy. It also features the studio of **Maurice Utrillo** and has a peaceful garden overlooking the city.

€14, not included in Museum Pass; good audioguide available.

Open Wed–Mon, 10:00–18:00 (last entry 45 minutes before closing).

Address: 12 Rue Cortot. Tel: +33 1 49 25 89 39.

While walking through Montmartre, look out for homes once occupied by **Picasso**, **Van Gogh**, **Erik Satie**, and **Toulouse-Lautrec**—simple buildings with plaques, easy to miss but rewarding to spot.

Further downhill, near **Métro Blanche**, you'll find the legendary **Moulin Rouge**, still running its over-the-top, high-priced shows with feathers, sequins, and champagne. The nearby **Au Lapin Agile** is still active, too, offering a more traditional cabaret experience. The area around **Pigalle** mixes sleaze and nightlife, with bars, music venues, and neon signs—the last bit of edgy Montmartre in today's Paris.

Père Lachaise Cemetery

Père Lachaise is the largest cemetery in Paris and perhaps the most famous in the world. It's not just a burial ground—it's a peaceful, tree-lined labyrinth of cobbled paths, ivy-covered tombs, and sculpted monuments that tell stories of art, music, literature, and love. Many visitors come not just to mourn but to reflect, explore, and experience this place as a monument to creativity and history.

Wander through its mini "neighborhoods" of gravestones, crypts, and mausoleums. A map is highly recommended and can be picked up for a couple of euros from florists near the **Porte Gambetta** entrance. Some of the most visited graves include:

- **Frédéric Chopin**, often adorned with flowers left by admirers
- **Oscar Wilde**, whose tomb is covered in graffiti messages and lipstick kisses
- **Jim Morrison**, whose grave has become a pilgrimage site for fans of The Doors
- **Édith Piaf**, the voice of Paris with a grave as humble as her beginnings
- **Molière**, the father of French comedy
- **Héloïse and Abélard**, medieval lovers buried side by side
- **Gertrude Stein and Alice B. Toklas**, inseparable even in death

Admission is **free**. Open Mon–Fri: 8:00–18:00; Sat: 8:30–18:00; Sun: 9:00–18:00 (winter hours may close earlier).

Don't use Métro Père Lachaise; instead, use **Métro Gambetta** and walk downhill.

Phone: +33 1 55 25 82 10.

Pompidou Center (Centre Georges Pompidou)

This bold, inside-out building, with its color-coded pipes and glass escalators, is impossible to miss. Love it or hate it, the **Pompidou Center** is one of the world's most important modern and contemporary art museums. The building itself is a statement, breaking with classical design to expose its infrastructure—air ducts, water pipes, and steel framing—on the outside.

Inside, you'll find five floors of galleries and spaces. The **permanent collection** on the 4th and 5th floors covers groundbreaking works from the 20th and 21st centuries—**Picasso, Braque, Kandinsky, Dali, Matisse, Duchamp**, and beyond. Each room offers a new twist on how to see the world, often challenging the very definition of art.

The top floor offers one of Paris' best panoramic views—especially stunning at sunset. If you don't want to tour the museum, you can still ride the external escalator to the **6th-floor lookout** for a smaller fee. The plaza out front often has street performers, food vendors, and people hanging out, giving the area a relaxed and artistic vibe.

Entry: €14 for permanent collection; free on the first Sunday of the month. €5 if you're only going for the escalator view.

Museum Pass covers permanent collection + terrace view.

Open Wed–Mon from 11:00 to 21:00 (building open later), closed Tuesday.

Avoid peak hours—come after 17:00 for smaller crowds.

Métro: **Rambuteau** or **Hôtel de Ville**.

Phone: +33 1 44 78 12 33.

Exploring the Marais

The Marais is the most elegant, historical and cultural part of all of the Paris neighborhoods. The twisting lanes, tiny museums, historic homes and assortment of boutiques and bakeries make it one of the finest places to walk. The name translates as "marsh," and in medieval times that's what it was. It was the 17th-century aristocrats who built their mansions here, and later waves of immigrants and a robust Jewish community that forged the neighborhood for generations.

The neighborhood retained its character while reinventing itself. Today it's an energetic mix of trendsetters, historians and locals, where kosher bakeries rub elbows with designer stores and falafel joints with art galleries, where weekend markets coexist with silent courtyards.

Begin your stroll at Place de la Bastille, and head west along Rue Saint-Antoine. You'll soon arrive at Place des Vosges, one of Paris' oldest and prettiest squares, surrounded by arcades and symmetry. From here, stroll into the Jewish Quarter along Rue des Rosiers, which is lined with bakeries, delis and Middle Eastern food counters.

After, wander along Rue des Francs-Bourgeois, famous for its shopping, and Rue Vieille du Temple, home to cafés and art spaces. The streets are lively and car-free on Sundays — ideal for an aimless afternoon of window-shopping and people-watching.

Be sure to visit the Shoah Memorial, a somber museum and monument to Holocaust victims, which lies on a quiet street nearby.

The **Marais** is also home to smaller museums worth visiting, like:

- **Musée Picasso**, filled with over 5,000 works by Picasso
- **Musée Cognacq-Jay**, with 18th-century art in a former private home
- **Archives Nationales**, with historical documents and exhibitions

It's a place where centuries overlap—and it's always changing while somehow staying the same.

Place des Vosges

This square is one of the most beautiful spots in Paris. It was constructed in 1605 under Henry IV and is the oldest planned square in the city. Locals love it. You'll spot parents talking on benches, youngsters running circles, pigeons pacing around and couples stretched out on the lawn. The vibe here is chilled out, calming and very Parisian.

The square itself is perfectly symmetrical, when lined with lovely arcades and red-brick buildings with gray slate roofs and rows of chimneys. Many of those bricks are touch-ups — painted on for symmetry — but they blend in so well you can't tell. Keep an eye out for the slightly taller buildings on the north and south ends — those used to be reserved for the king and queen, who never actually moved in.

In the center is a statue of Louis XIII on horseback (installed by his son in homage to his dad). Along the edges, the arcades are lined with cafés, small shops and art galleries. You could buy a coffee, sit under the arches and just enjoy the atmosphere.

At **number 6**, you'll find **Victor Hugo's old home**, now a small museum. It's free and worth popping into, especially if you've read *Les Misérables* or *The Hunchback of Notre Dame*.

Victor Hugo's House (Maison de Victor Hugo)

This is where Hugo lived from 1832 to 1848, and it's a surprisingly personal museum. The rooms are arranged to reflect key phases of his life—from his early fame to his long exile and final years as a national hero. You'll see original furniture, family photos, paintings, and items that bring Hugo's world to life.

There are English signs throughout, so it's easy to follow, even if you don't know much about French literature. It's a quiet, thoughtful visit—small and not too crowded.

It's open **Tuesday to Sunday**, 10:00 to 18:00, Free to enter, though there's a charge for temporary exhibits. There's a cute little café in the courtyard if you need a break.

Address: **6 Place des Vosges**

Métro: **Bastille**, **Saint-Paul**, or **Chemin Vert**

Picasso Museum (Musée Picasso)

Whether you like Picasso or not, this museum provides a good overview of his wild, creative path. It's in a stately old mansion and displays paintings, drawings, sculptures and personal effects from various phases of his career. The exhibits change frequently, so it's always a little bit different.

The museum does an excellent job of signage in French and English, and the space itself is bright and welcoming. It's a good way to take in how Picasso's work shifted over time — not to mention some of the lesser-known stuff.

Open **Tuesday to Sunday**, generally from late morning to early evening. It's **€14** and included in the **Museum Pass**.

Address: **5 Rue de Thorigny**

Métro access: St-**Sébastien–Froissart**, **St-Paul**, or **Chemin Vert stations**

Jewish Art and History Museum

Dedicated to the life, traditions, and resilience of the Jewish people throughout Europe and France, this museum is found on the Marais district. Even if you don't really know Jewish history, the exhibits and audioguide make everything clear and meaningful. You will see ceremonial objects, textiles, old manuscripts and art, and moving sections on the Holocaust and postwar life.

It's located in a beautiful old mansion, and the collection is well organized. People who know a little about Judaism will get a lot out of it — but even if you're just curious, it's a great stop.

Admission is **€10**, including the audioguide, and it's on the **Museum Pass**. Free on the **first Saturday of each month** from October through June.

Open **Tuesday to Sunday**; closed Mondays.

Address: **71 Rue du Temple**

Métro: **Rambuteau** or **Hôtel de Ville**

Paris Day Trips

Versailles

A train ride from Paris away, Versailles is one of the most jaw dropping palace experiences in the world. Constructed to impress and subjugate, this vast estate is where Louis XIV, the "Sun King," built a symbol of absolute monarchy that still dazzles visitors today.

Why Go?

Versailles is more than a palace — it's a whole world. Within the estate are royal apartments, grand halls, extensive gardens with fountains, the Trianon palaces and Marie-Antoinette's lovely hamlet. It's overwhelming but also unforgettable."

Visit for the glamour, the history and the sheer scale of it all. Remain to envision the life of court of those kings and queens who once resided here in full costume, wigs and powdered faces.

What to See

The Château (Main Palace): Stroll through the magnificent Hall of Mirrors, the Royal Chapel, the King's and Queen's Apartments and ornate salons. Every room is a story of royal opulence and political force.

Gardens and Fountains: The formal French gardens span several miles, with sculptures, tree-lined walks and ornate fountains. On fountain show days (weekends and some Tuesdays, April–October), music plays and water dances — plan around this if you want the full effect.

Grand and Petit Trianon Palaces Smaller, more cozy retreats once used by kings, later by Marie-Antoinette. They reveal another aspect of life at court — stylish and rather less formal.

Marie-Antoinette's Hamlet: A storybook hamlet built for the queen to avoid life at the palace. There's a dairy, mill, vegetable gardens and tiny farmhouses. It's quiet and slightly surreal.

Getting There

Take the RER C train (around 35 minutes) from stations including St-Michel, Musée d'Orsay or Champ de Mars. Get a round-trip ticket to Versailles Château – Rive Gauche (~€ 7.60). The main gate is a 10-minute walk from the station. Follow the signs, and the crowds.

You can also book a guided tour or join a small group. It is more expensive but can help you skip lines and understand better what you're seeing.

Hours and Tickets

- **Château:** Tue–Sun 9:00–18:30 (last entry at 17:45). Closed Mondays.

- **Gardens:** Open daily; free on most days (ticketed on fountain show days).

- **Trianon and Domaine:** Noon–18:30. Closed Mondays.

Tickets:

- €20 for the Palace only

- €30–€32 for the **Passport** (access to all areas, including gardens on show days)

- **Free** first Sunday of the month (Nov–March)

- **Paris Museum Pass** holders must still **reserve a time slot** online

- Book online at: www.chateauversailles.fr

Crowd Tips

- Avoid weekends and Tuesdays (since many Paris museums are closed that day).

- Arrive by **8:30** to line up for 9:00 entry.

- Start with the palace interior, then do the gardens and Trianons after lunch.

- Bring snacks or buy food at the cafés near the Grand Canal.

Getting Around

- Walking the full estate takes time.

- **Petit train:** €8.50 round trip, good for tired legs.

- **Bike rentals** near the Grand Canal: €9/hour

- **Golf carts:** €38/hour, follow a set route. Not allowed at Trianon.

Tips

- Wear comfy shoes—there's lots of walking.

- Bring water, especially in summer.

- On cooler days, layers are key—the gardens can get breezy.

- Allow a full **day** to explore. It's worth it.

Chartres

A tranquil getaway from Paris, Chartres is far enough away to feel like a break from the city — but close enough for an easy day trip. Not far from 90 km (55 miles) southwest of Paris, it is a picturesque town focused around an impressive cathedral and quiet, medieval streets.

Why Go?

Chartres is known for its Cathédrale Notre-Dame, one of Europe's finest examples of High Gothic architecture. It's not merely a church — it's a work of art. The cathedral, completed between 1194 and 1250, has endured wars, revolutions and the ravages of time itself.

You don't have to be an architecture lover to be moved by this place. The exterior is huge and ornate, with two outsize, mismatched spires, flying buttresses and carved doorways. The real magic, though, is within: stained-glass windows that shimmer in deep blue, ruby red and gold, many of them dating back to the 12th and 13th centuries.

Beyond the cathedral, the town is peaceful and beautiful. A few quiet streets, small shops, relaxed cafés and a riverbank walkway make it conducive to wandering and taking your time. It's the kind of place where you can take a little deeper breath.

What to See

Chartres Cathedral (Cathédrale Notre-Dame): The main event. Admission is free, and the building is open daily, from 8:30 to 19:30. Be sure to check out the famed Blue Virgin window, the Jesse Tree, and the massive rose windows. There's a small charge to visit the crypt and tower, which provide more-depth insights and great views.

Labyrinth on the Floor: Within the nave is a 13-meter-wide labyrinth set into the floor — pilgrim travelers walked this way as a symbolic journey. It's usually shrouded in chairs but uncovered on Fridays (and some summer days).

Light Show (Chartres en Lumières): From mid-April to early October, buildings across the town are illuminated in vivid projections after dusk each evening—including the cathedral façade. It's free, quiet and magical."

Walking the Old Town: Stroll through winding alleys, alongside half-timbered homes and the placid Eure River. Bring a snack and relax by the water. Everything is nearby and walkable.

Getting There

Trains run frequently from **Gare Montparnasse** to Chartres (about one hour, €16–€20 each way). No reservation is required—just show up and grab a seat. From the station, it's a 10-minute walk to the cathedral. Easy and direct.

Good to Know

Entry to the cathedral is **free**, but there's a small charge for crypt and tower access.

There are **free guided tours** in English during the high season (usually April–October)—check the cathedral's website or tourist office for schedules.

The **Tourist Information Office** is just across from the cathedral, useful for maps and updated info.

Tips

Visit in the **morning** to see the windows lit by natural sunlight.

Spring and early fall are great for avoiding both heat and crowds.

Don't rush—this is a place to slow down, walk, and look up.

Giverny (Monet's Garden)

If you've ever admired Monet's dreamy water lilies and wondered what inspired them, make a pilgrimage to Giverny. Only 50 miles west of Paris, this small village is where Claude Monet lived and painted for more than 40 years. His home and garden have become a pilgrimage site for art lovers — and they are worth the hype.

Why Go?

Giverny is not only for Impressionist aficionados. It's a serene flower-filled site that exemplifies the character of the French countryside. Walking through Monet's garden is like wandering into one of his paintings: vibrant flower beds, an arched green footbridge, lily draped ponds, pathways that beg for leisurely, contemplative strolls.

The garden is divided in two: the Clos Normand, in front of the house (overflowing with flowers from spring through fall), and the famed Water Garden, across the road, which contain the Japanese bridge and water lilies that figure in some of his most well-known works.

Monet's pink home feels both bright and playful. You can wander through his cobalt-blue kitchen, sunflower-yellow dining room and cozy sitting room — all preserved, with period furniture and reproductions of his treasured Japanese prints.

What to See

The Water Garden: Duck through a short tunnel under the road to the pond. The wisteria-covered curved bridge and lily-planted still water make this the highlight for many. It's serene but well-trafficked, so for fewer crowds, arrive in the early morning or late afternoon.

The Flower Garden: Rows of seasonal blooms — tulips, roses, irises and dahlias — line the path. Every pathway opens up to color and surprise. This section continuously shifts with the seasons.

Monet's Home: Intimate and on the small side, the home offers insight into Monet's simple life. Note: Original paintings are not on view here, but the ambience makes up for that.

Musée des Impressionnismes Giverny: This small museum, just a stroll from the house, has rotating exhibitions about Impressionism and Monet's contemporaries.

Practical Info

Getting There: Trains leave from Paris' Gare St-Lazare to Vernon (45 minutes, about €30 round-trip). From Vernon, take a shuttle bus (€10 round-trip), taxi (around €20 one-way), or rent a bike from a café near the station for a scenic 6 km ride. Giverny is well-marked and bike-friendly.

Hours & Prices: The house and gardens are open daily from late March to early November, 9:30–18:00 (last entry at 17:30). Entry: €11 (not covered by the Paris

Museum Pass). Children under 7 enter free. Combo tickets with the Impressionist museum are available.

Tips for Visiting:

- Arrive early or late in the day to avoid tour groups.

- Spring (April–May) and early fall (September) are ideal times, but even summer is worth it if you're prepared for crowds.

- Don't rush. Giverny is small, and part of the magic is just sitting on a bench and soaking in the garden.

Fontainebleau

If you're up for a day trip that's historical (more so than Versailles, actually), less touristy and full of forested charm, going to Fontainebleau is in order. Less than an hour away from Paris by train, it offers an easy and peaceful getaway from the city.

Why Go?

Fonts is all about space, style and atmosphere. The Château de Fontainebleau was a royal residence for over seven centuries, making it feel more like a lived-in palace than a film set. It's where Napoleon Bonaparte bid farewell to his troops before his exile. But even before him, kings and queens strode through these halls — and each left their imprint in evolving styles, wings and furnishings.

Whereas Versailles dazzles with cavernous scale and formal symmetry, Fontainebleau seems more intimate. It is richly decorated but less formal, amid quiet gardens and a woods that was once used for royal hunting.

What to See

Within the château, wander through countless furnished rooms, such as the grand Renaissance halls of François I, opulent apartments of Napoleon and the sole throne room remaining in France. Don't skip the Gallery of Francis I, with its richly carved walls and paintings, a highlight of 16th-century art.

The château's grounds are a highlight as well: spacious open courtyards, landscaped gardens, fountains and long walkways, but far fewer crowds than Versailles. You can walk around freely or sit down on a bench in silence under the trees.

Right beyond the château is the forest of Fontainebleau, a vast natural expanse perfect for hiking, bouldering or simply wandering through the shaded boughs of ancient oak trees.

Practical Info

Getting There: Take a direct train (Transilien Line R) from Gare de Lyon to Fontainebleau-Avon station (about 40 minutes). From the station, a local bus or short taxi ride takes you to the château (about 2.5 km).

Château Hours & Prices: Open every day except Tuesday. October to March: 9:30–17:00. April to September: 9:30–18:00. The last entry is 45 minutes before closing. Entry costs around €13; included in the Paris Museum Pass.

Local Tips:

- Avoid Mondays (some rooms and services may be closed), and try to visit on a weekday to skip school groups.

- Bring water and maybe some snacks. There are cafés nearby, but options are limited inside the grounds.

- If the weather's nice, pack a picnic and find a quiet spot in the gardens or by the carp pond.

A Page of History (Quick and Casual Overview)

Ancient Roots (A.D. 1–1500)

Julius Caesar conquered Paris when it was a mere Gallic settlement, and it's been a momentum from there. This intermixing of Roman and Celtic culture is what created the French identity. Then came the Normans, then the Franks — hence "France." Charlemagne brought the Franks together for a time, and in 1066, French and English interests collided, courtesy of William the Conqueror. Later on, Joan of Arc rallied the French to drive the British out.

Golden Age (1500–1799)

This was France's big rise. Under its kings François I and Louis XIV (the Sun King), France assumed the role of trendsetter in Europe. French became the language of the elite, and Versailles was a showcase of both the country's power and wealth. From art to fashion, all sought inspiration from France.

The French Revolution (1789–1800)

It all began to unravel in 1789, when the people stormed the Bastille. The king and queen were executed, and the guillotine became a staple. From that chaos emerged a new leader — Napoleon Bonaparte.

Napoleon and the 1800s

Napoleon crowned himself emperor and dominated much of Europe before crashing badly in Russia. Monarchs came back after that, but under new democratic pressures. The remainder of the century was a wild mix of art and invention, and flash in Parisian life. The Eiffel Tower went up. Impressionist art bloomed. Something was booming in the belle époque.

Global Wars and Recovery Plan (1900–1950s)

France took a huge hit in WWI then got steamrolled in WWII. Paris was occupied but later freed. In the meantime, artists like Hemingway and Picasso had Paris as their playground.

Modern France (1950–Now)

And Charles de Gaulle oversaw the country's reconstruction. France lost its colonies but emerged as a force in modern Europe. Through political change and waves of immigration, Paris grew into a vibrant, multicultural capital. Today, it's one of the world's great destinations, blending old magnificence with contemporary life.

TOP EXPERIENCES

There's no shortage of things to do in Paris beyond museums and monuments. This chapter highlights the best ways to explore the city—by boat, bus, bike, or on foot. Whether you're into food, history, or just soaking up the atmosphere, there's something for everyone.

A simple Seine cruise is one of the easiest ways to enjoy Paris from a new angle. You can also hop on a bus tour for a big-picture view of the city or join a walking or bike tour to dig deeper into the stories and streets that make Paris unique.

Markets and side streets are often overlooked by people rushing between landmarks. But if you slow down and explore local neighborhoods, you'll see a completely different side of the city—one where real Parisians live, shop, and relax. And make sure to leave some energy for the evening. Paris at night is magical: lit-up bridges, concerts in chapels, quiet strolls, or a late glass of wine at a café.

City Tours

Hop-On, Hop-Off Sightseeing Buses

For a laid-back way to get your bearings, climb aboard one of Paris's iconic double-decker tour buses. These open-air vehicles follow scenic circuits that pass by the city's major attractions. You can jump off to explore whenever a stop interests you and rejoin the route at your own pace. It's especially enjoyable on a sunny day, making it a great pick for your first outing. Keep in mind that traffic can be a drawback, and if you're eager to maximize your time, the Métro might get you places faster. Expect to pay around €36–39. One of the most central options is Tootbus's 10-stop loop (tootbus.com), which covers all the must-sees.

Cruising the Seine

Drift past Paris's most celebrated landmarks on a relaxing boat ride down the Seine. Several companies run one-hour cruises for €15–17, offering up-close views of monuments like the Eiffel Tower, Notre-Dame, and the Louvre. Evening cruises are particularly enchanting, with the city's architecture beautifully lit against the night sky. Looking for a more intimate or romantic option? Opt for a twilight sailing. Bateaux-Mouches is the largest operator, with departures from Pont de l'Alma, though their massive boats can feel crowded. For a cozier ride, consider Bateaux Parisiens or Vedettes de Paris (near the Eiffel Tower), or Vedettes du Pont Neuf, which departs—no surprise—from Pont Neuf.

Explore on Foot with a Guide

If you prefer learning while you wander, consider joining a guided walking tour. It's a great way to uncover the history, art, and culture hidden in plain sight. Paris Walks (paris-walks.com) offers fun and informative two-hour tours in English, priced between €15 and €25. For those who crave deeper insights—especially in subjects like art history or French cuisine—Context Travel (contexttravel.com) curates expert-led experiences in small groups, starting at around €120.

Fat Tire Guided Tours

For something more casual and upbeat, Fat Tire Tours is a solid choice. They lead both bike and walking tours around the city (typically Mondays, Wednesdays, and Fridays at 10:00 a.m. or 3:00 p.m.) as well as specialized outings to spots like Versailles or Sainte-Chapelle. Many of their tours include fast-track entry to busy attractions like the Eiffel Tower or the Catacombs—an excellent perk during peak seasons. Visit fattiretours.com/paris for current offerings, availability, and discounts (like €2 off per ticket, up to two people). Their office is located on Rue Edgar Faure.

Living the Local Way

Paris is more than a city full of sights—it's a place to meet real people and experience how life works here. That's what makes a trip more personal and memorable. You don't have to be a fluent French speaker to connect with locals. There are lots of ways to meet Parisians and share a slice of daily life.

Start with **Paris Greeters**. These are local volunteers who'll take you on free, informal walks through their neighborhoods—no tip is expected, just good conversation. You can learn about their favorite cafés, quiet parks, and how they see the city. It's like hanging out with a Parisian friend for a few hours (parisgreeters.fr).

In the **Rue Cler area**, the **Franco-American Center** and **the American Church in Paris** (at 65 Quai d'Orsay) offer English-speaking services, gatherings, concerts, and meetups. Both are great spots for travelers who want to feel a little more plugged into the local community.

If you love food, **Paris by Mouth** runs small-group food tours (mostly in English) that take you through markets and bakeries, tasting cheeses, wines, and pastries along the way. You'll learn a ton and eat very well. Want to cook something yourself? **La Cuisine Paris** teaches hands-on classes for everything from French bread to macarons and full meals—fun and accessible, no experience needed (lacuisineparis.com).

For something a little different, check out **Lost in Frenchlation**, which hosts French movie nights with English subtitles—perfect for seeing French cinema without language stress. They often screen films in cool old theaters and serve drinks beforehand (lostinfrenchlation.com).

Wine fans should head to **Ô Château**, a wine-tasting space inside an 18th-century home once owned by Madame de Pompadour. Tastings are casual, informative, and available in English. You'll leave with a better sense of French wine—and probably a bit tipsy (o-chateau.com).

Hiring a Guide

Sometimes, it's worth hiring a local guide for a half-day, especially if you want a deeper look at art, history, or culture. Good private guides charge around €240–300 per half day. For qualified, English-speaking experts, check out french-guide.com.

Biking Around Paris

Exploring Paris by bike is easier than it sounds, and it's a great way to see more without rushing. Two solid options:

Bike About Tours offers relaxed rides through less-touristy areas like the Marais, Latin Quarter, and Ile Saint-Louis. Their **Hidden Paris Tour** (about 3.5 hours) shows you places most visitors miss. €45 per person, with a small discount through Rick Steves. They're based at 17 Rue du Pont Louis Philippe, near Hôtel de Ville (Mo: St-Paul). Book at bikeabouttours.com, or text them: +33 6 18 80 84 92.

Fat Tire Tours runs lively three-hour bike tours past major sights like the Eiffel Tower and the Louvre (€39–44). Their evening rides are especially popular—see the city lit up at night and end with a Seine cruise (€44). The night ride runs daily 18:30 from May to August. Their office is on Rue Edgar Faure, close to the Eiffel Tower (Mo: Dupleix or La Motte-Picquet-Grenelle). More info at fattiretours.com, or call +33 1 82 88 80 96.

Paris Shopping Guide

Shopping in Paris isn't just about buying stuff—it's a part of the culture. You're not just browsing shelves; you're stepping into traditions, chatting with shopkeepers, and walking through centuries of design, fashion, and craftsmanship. From famous department stores to quiet corner bakeries, it's about the atmosphere as much as the goods.

How to Shop Like a Local

In smaller shops or boutiques, polite greetings go a long way. Always say *"Bonjour, Madame"* or *"Bonjour, Monsieur"* when entering, and *"Merci, au revoir"* when you leave. It's a simple courtesy and makes the interaction much smoother. If you want to browse quietly, a polite *"Je regarde, merci"* (I'm just looking, thank you) is enough. Always ask before touching something, especially in smaller or high-end stores—*"Je peux?"* (Can I?) is short and clear.

When Shops Are Open

Most shops open around 10:00 and close at 19:00. Some take a lunch break from 13:00 to 15:00. Many close on Sundays, except in areas like the Marais or near tourist spots. Department stores and chains usually stay open, but always double-check if you're planning a shopping trip on Sunday or Monday, as hours vary more than you might expect.

Where to Find Souvenirs

For those classic Parisian souvenirs—Eiffel Tower keychains, vintage postcards, books, or mini prints of Monet—start near Notre-Dame. The green bookstalls along the Seine (called *bouquinistes*) have a lot of character and make great browsing stops. Rue d'Arcole is lined with shops selling postcards, snow globes, and everything in between. Around Montmartre, you'll find plenty of street artists selling sketches and paintings, often just off Place du Tertre. Inside many large department stores, you'll also find dedicated souvenir sections with better-curated gifts like books, scarves, or teas.

Department Stores: Classic and Convenient

Paris invented the department store, and it shows. The two big ones—**Galeries Lafayette** and **Printemps**—are both located on Boulevard Haussmann. Galeries Lafayette has a stunning stained-glass dome, fashion brands across all budgets, a gourmet food hall, and a rooftop terrace with free panoramic views. Just across the street, Printemps leans more toward affordable fashion and has a good rooftop café.

For something quieter but just as Parisian, **Le Bon Marché** on the Left Bank (in the Sèvres-Babylone area) is the oldest department store in Paris. It's known for being elegant without being showy, and it's especially good for gourmet food and home goods. Its food hall, **La Grande Épicerie**, is a great stop for picking up beautifully packaged edible souvenirs—chocolates, wine, jams, pâtés, and more.

Luxury and Foodie Shopping: Place de la Madeleine to Rue St-Honoré

This area between **Place de la Madeleine** and **Place Vendôme** is like a playground for serious shoppers. You'll find gourmet institutions like **Maison de la Truffe**, **Mariage Frères** for tea, and **La Maison du Chocolat**. The former Fauchon corner has been reinvented as a luxury café and shop. Follow **Rue Royale** to **Rue St-Honoré** for top designer stores, including **Chanel**, **Goyard**, and **Colette** (which closed in 2017 but left a huge style legacy). Finish at the elegant **Place Vendôme**, home to high-end jewelry brands like Cartier and Boucheron.

Street Markets and Food Shopping

Many Paris neighborhoods have weekly *marchés* (outdoor food markets). These aren't just for locals—they're fantastic for visitors who want a picnic or just a cultural experience. Vendors often offer samples, and you'll find everything from goat cheese to fresh figs. Here are a few to check out:

- **Rue Cler** (7th arrondissement): A charming street market open nearly every day, with bakeries, butchers, cheese shops, and cafés.

- **Rue Mouffetard** (5th): A bustling market street with deep roots in Parisian history.

- **Marché Bastille** (11th): Huge market on Thursdays and Sundays with food, clothes, and crafts.

- **Marché d'Aligre** (12th): One of the city's most vibrant and multicultural markets—part open-air, part covered.

Even if you're not buying, walking through these markets offers insight into local life and flavors.

Flea Markets

- **Marché aux Puces de St-Ouen**: Paris' most famous flea market (open Sat–Mon) just north of the city. It's a maze of antiques, art, vintage clothes, and collectibles. Don't rush—this place takes time to explore.

- **Marché de Vanves**: Smaller and more manageable, but with great finds, open Sat and Sun morning. It's more local and less overwhelming, and prices are sometimes better.

Pro tip: Bargaining is okay at flea markets, especially if you're buying multiple items. A polite *"Vous pouvez faire un petit prix?"* (Can you give me a small discount?) can work wonders.

Hidden Shopping Streets

Beyond the big names, there are charming shopping streets worth walking just for the vibe:

- **Rue Montorgueil**: Food-focused and lively, near Les Halles.

- **Rue de Buci and Rue de Seine**: Left Bank classics full of small shops, wine stores, and cozy cafés.

- **Rue des Francs-Bourgeois**: In the Marais, with a mix of boutiques, galleries, and big-name brands, and open on Sundays.

- **Passages Couverts**: Covered arcades like **Passage des Panoramas** or **Galerie Vivienne**, with bookstores, vintage shops, and tearooms—perfect for rainy days.

Seasonal Events & Festivals

Paris is lively all year, but each season brings its own energy and special events. Whether you're into food, fashion, art, or music, the city always has something happening. Some festivals are small and local, others are massive international gatherings—but they all offer an easy, authentic way to connect with the city.

Spring (March–May)

This is when Paris shakes off the winter chill. Trees bloom, café terraces fill up, and people return to parks and riversides.

- **Nuit des Musées (May):** One night a year, Paris museums stay open late and free—often until midnight—with special exhibits, music, and tours. A great way to explore places like the Louvre or Orsay with a different atmosphere.

- **Foire de Paris (late April–early May):** A massive fair at the Porte de Versailles expo center, with food tastings, home goods, and inventions—mostly local, very lively.

- **Printemps des Rues:** A street arts festival in the Canal St-Martin area with free outdoor performances: circus acts, dance, music, and more.

Summer (June–August)

Summer is full of festivals and long evenings. Locals go on vacation in August, so parts of the city feel quieter—though the tourist zones stay active.

- **Fête de la Musique (June 21):** On the longest day of the year, Paris turns into one giant, open-air concert. Every neighborhood has musicians on the street—amateur and pro, from classical to techno. It's loud, chaotic, and a lot of fun.

- **Paris Plages (mid-July to late August):** The banks of the Seine and some canals are turned into mini beach resorts with sand, umbrellas, games, and events—completely free.

- **Bastille Day (July 14):** France's national holiday. Expect a morning military parade on the Champs-Élysées, jets flying overhead, and a huge fireworks show at the Eiffel Tower at night. The whole city celebrates. Many museums and shops are closed that day.

- **Cinéma en Plein Air (July–August):** Free open-air movies in parks like Parc de la Villette. Bring a blanket, a bottle of wine, and settle in under the stars.

all (September–November)

The weather cools, locals return to work and school, and the city starts to feel more Parisian again.

- **Journées du Patrimoine (Heritage Days, mid-September):** For one weekend, usually the third weekend of September, hundreds of buildings usually closed to the public open their doors—palaces, ministries, private mansions, and more.

- **Nuit Blanche (early October):** Contemporary art takes over Paris for one night. Museums and galleries stay open, and artists install large-scale works all over the city—from bridges to train stations.

- **Montmartre Wine Harvest (early October):** Yes, Paris has its vineyard! The Fête des Vendanges in Montmartre celebrates the grape harvest with a parade, wine tasting, fireworks, and lots of music.

Winter (December–February)

Even in the cold, Paris keeps going—with Christmas lights, indoor markets, and warm cafés.

- **Christmas Markets (late November–December):** Little wooden chalets pop up across the city—Tuileries Garden, Notre-Dame, Saint-Germain. They sell snacks, hot wine, handmade gifts, and more. Great for browsing and warming up.

- **New Year's Eve (December 31):** Most people celebrate with dinner and drinks. Crowds gather at the Champs-Élysées or under the Eiffel Tower to watch the midnight light show. There's no official fireworks display, but the atmosphere is festive.

- **Chinese New Year (late Jan or Feb):** Celebrated big in the 13th arrondissement with parades, lion dances, music, and food. One of the most colorful winter events.

Parks and Gardens

Paris isn't just museums and monuments—it's also full of beautiful green spaces where locals relax, read, picnic, or just people-watch. Whether you want a quiet bench under the trees or a lively playground surrounded by fountains, there's a park for every mood.

Luxembourg Garden (Jardin du Luxembourg)

This is the heart of Left Bank leisure. With tidy flowerbeds, shady chestnut trees, fountains, statues, and green chairs all around, it's one of the best places to sit and take it slow. Kids sail toy boats on the central pond, play on the playground, or ride ponies. There are also tennis courts, chess boards, and a bandstand with concerts in summer.

The French Senate is housed in the palace here, and it's still in use—so the garden is very well maintained.

Tuileries Garden (Jardin des Tuileries)

Between the Louvre and Place de la Concorde, this classic garden was designed by the same team that created Versailles. Long gravel paths, rows of statues, fountains with metal chairs around them—this is where locals and tourists both stop to rest. It's ideal for a break during a museum day. Kids love the summer fair with rides and games.

Palais Royal Garden

Hidden just behind the Louvre, this peaceful, symmetrical garden is often missed by tourists. Surrounded by arcades and lined with elegant trees and benches, it feels private and calm. Locals come here to read, chat, or enjoy lunch. It's one of the city's most elegant spots—and the black-and-white Colonnes de Buren art installation is also here.

Champ de Mars

The grassy field stretching out from the Eiffel Tower is one of the top picnic spots in town. It's big and open, with plenty of views of the tower. Best for evening picnics when the tower sparkles every hour after dark. There are also playgrounds, bike lanes, and plenty of space to spread out.

Parc des Buttes-Chaumont

In northeastern Paris, this one's off the usual tourist path. It's hilly and wild-looking, with cliffs, waterfalls, suspension bridges, and a dramatic temple on a high rock. More locals than tourists come here—often couples or groups of friends hanging out on the grass with food and drinks. Great for a break from the city center.

Parc Monceau

In the fancy 8th arrondissement, Parc Monceau is quieter and elegant, with curved paths, romantic statues, a little pond, and even a few fake ruins. It's great for reading under the trees or watching well-dressed locals jog and walk their dogs.

Bois de Vincennes and Bois de Boulogne

These are Paris's two biggest parks—more like forests at the edge of the city. The Bois de Vincennes, in the east, has a zoo, flower gardens, and lakes with rowboats. The Bois de Boulogne, in the west, is home to the Fondation Louis Vuitton museum, a large lake, and paths for walking and biking. These are good for long strolls or even full-day escapes.

VAT Refund and Duty Rules

If you're a non-EU resident and you shop in Paris, you may be able to get a partial refund of the VAT (Value-Added Tax), which is built into the price of most items. This tax is around 20 to 21 percent, and the refund applies only to physical goods—not to services like hotel stays, meals, or transportation. To qualify, you have to spend at least €175 in a single day at one store. Some high-end boutiques and large department stores like Galeries Lafayette or Printemps are very familiar with the process and will print out the necessary tax refund forms for you at checkout.

When you're ready to pay, ask the store if they offer détaxe or tax-free shopping. If they do, they'll usually need to see your passport, and they'll give you a form with your purchase information. When you leave the country, you must have these forms stamped by customs at the airport, so make sure to carry the goods in your carry-on if possible. The items should be unused and available for inspection. After clearing customs and getting the form validated—often by scanning it at a kiosk—you can either drop it in a box for processing or take it to a counter operated by refund companies like Global Blue or Planet. Refunds can be given as cash (euros), returned to your credit card, or sent by check. The refund process can take a few weeks if you choose the card option.

Keep in mind that without the official customs stamp or scan at departure, the refund will not be processed. If your form isn't submitted within 3 months of purchase, it becomes invalid.

If you're flying back to the United States, there are customs limits to be aware of. Americans can bring back up to $800 worth of goods per person every 30 days without paying any duty. That amount includes everything you buy—clothing, souvenirs, or gifts. If you go over, the extra is usually taxed at a low flat rate. In addition, each adult may bring back one liter of alcohol and a limited amount of tobacco products duty-free. Items must be declared upon arrival, so keep all receipts and be prepared to show them to the customs officer if asked.

More detailed and updated information is available on the U.S. Customs and Border Protection website at www.help.cbp.gov.

VAT Refund and Customs for UK and Canadian Travelers

If you live outside the EU, including the UK or Canada, you can get a refund on the 20% VAT included in most prices in France—mainly for clothes, cosmetics, electronics, and other goods (not meals or services). You need to spend over €175 in one store, in one day, and ask the shop for a tax refund form (called "détaxe"). Show your passport at checkout. Before you leave the EU, scan the form at a customs kiosk (usually at the airport) and either drop it in the box provided or go to a refund desk. Refunds can be made to your card, by check, or in cash.

UK residents can bring home up to £390 worth of goods duty-free. If you go over, you may have to pay tax. Canadians can bring back CAN$800 worth of goods per person after seven days abroad or CAN$200 for shorter trips. Alcohol and tobacco limits apply. Check your country's customs website before travel for full details.

Evening Entertainment

Paris becomes something else entirely after dark. The streets are quieter, the monuments are lit, and the whole city seems to exhale. One of the most memorable ways to enjoy a Parisian evening is to stretch out dinner, then take a stroll through the glowing old streets. Wander past fountains, pause in the squares, and just let the city pull you along.

Jazz and Blues

Paris has long been a second home for jazz, especially for American musicians who found freedom and inspiration here after WWII. You'll find great live music all over town—sometimes elegant, sometimes underground, sometimes spontaneous. One classic venue is Caveau de la Huchette in the Latin Quarter, where a vaulted cellar hosts nightly jazz and dancing. It's a sweaty, low-ceilinged place that hasn't changed much in decades. Over on Rue des Lombards, Au Duc des Lombards offers a more polished vibe with serious musicians and a small theater feel. Just next door, Le Sunside and Le Sunset (they share the same space but alternate shows) are great for smaller sets, rising talent, and a relaxed crowd. Most shows cost €12–€25, and set times vary. If you're unsure where to go, check current lineups on Paris Voice.

Classical Music in Churches

If jazz isn't your thing, churches across the city host intimate classical concerts almost nightly. Some of the most atmospheric venues are Sainte-Chapelle, where you can hear Mozart or Vivaldi while surrounded by towering stained glass; St. Sulpice with its powerful organ; and the cozy and very old St. Julien-le-Pauvre near Notre Dame. Concerts usually cost €20–€35 and last about an hour. Sainte-Chapelle gets chilly in colder months, so bring a jacket even in spring.

Opera and Ballet

If you want something grander, check out the schedule at Opéra Bastille for modern productions with impressive staging. For an old-world experience, step into the historic Opéra Garnier with its marble staircases and painted ceilings. They still host performances—both opera and ballet—and even if you're not seeing a show, you can book a daytime visit to explore the building. Tickets often sell out, so it's smart to reserve online in advance.

Museums at Night

Several museums stay open late once or twice a week. These late-night hours—called visites nocturnes—are perfect if you want to avoid the daytime crowds. The Pompidou, Orsay, and sometimes the Louvre extend their hours into the evening. Wandering through Monet's water lilies or Rodin's sculptures at night can be an entirely different experience. Check individual museum websites for updated late-night schedules.

Evening Shows at Versailles

On certain summer Saturday nights, Versailles hosts Les Grandes Eaux Nocturnes, a fountain and light show in the gardens. Expect fireworks, music, mist, and a surreal walk through hedges and sculptures after dark. It's crowded but worth it.

Night Tours

There's something special about seeing Paris from the backseat of a car, especially when it's quiet and lit up. Some companies offer guided rides in classic Citroën 2CVs—tiny cars with soft tops and a lot of charm. These tours are pricey, around €90–€150 for a ride of about 1.5 hours, but it's a unique way to experience the city. A cheaper option is simply hiring a regular taxi or an Uber to do a loop: Notre Dame, Left Bank, Eiffel Tower, Place de la Concorde, Champs-Élysées, and back. A one-hour ride costs around €40–€50, depending on traffic. You can also book a sunset or nighttime Seine cruise for a more peaceful ride past all the landmarks, lit up along the water.

Places to Be at Night

The view from Place du Trocadéro is always stunning after dark. Street performers, couples, food vendors—it's busy but magical. From there, walk toward the Eiffel Tower, which sparkles every hour on the hour. The Champs-Élysées also shines at night, especially the view looking up toward the Arc de Triomphe. For something more relaxed, cross over to the Ile St. Louis, grab an ice cream from Berthillon if it's still open, and walk along the river toward Notre Dame. This part of the city is romantic, peaceful, and feels untouched by time.

The Left Bank also comes alive at night, especially in Saint-Germain-des-Prés. Around Rue de Buci and Rue des Canettes, you'll find a blend of classic bistros, wine bars, jazz clubs, and cinemas. It's lively but less chaotic than other parts of the city.

Montmartre is beautiful at night, though you should be cautious, especially around Pigalle, which still holds its old red-light district reputation. For a very old-school night, try Au Lapin Agile, a cabaret that feels like a time capsule—wooden chairs, candlelight, and French songs (€35 per person, French only). It's tucked behind the Sacré-Cœur on a quiet street and makes for a lovely finish to a nighttime walk through the hilltop village.

ACCOMMODATIONS

Where you sleep in Paris matters almost as much as what hotel you choose. Picking the right neighborhood will shape your whole experience. Some areas are picturesque but sleepy. Others are charming during the day but get loud at night. Some are central but overrun with tourists. It's all about balance—and matching the location to your travel style.

I usually recommend staying in one of three areas: **Rue Cler, the Marais, or the Luxembourg neighborhood**.

- **Rue Cler** is a postcard-perfect market street just steps from the Eiffel Tower. It's quiet at night, filled with food shops and cafés during the day, and well connected to transit.

- **The Marais**, on the Right Bank, is fun, creative, stylish, and full of history— great for evening walks, boutique shopping, and people-watching. Think art galleries, falafel shops, and cobbled alleys.

- **The Luxembourg area**, on the Left Bank, feels more local and elegant. You're near gardens, bookstores, and cafés full of students, professionals, and neighbors rather than tourists.

Other options: the peaceful **Île St. Louis** (romantic but pricey), the youthful **Rue Mouffetard** area (village vibes near the Latin Quarter), and **Montmartre** (hilltop charm and creative history, but with some uphill walking and occasional crowds).

What to Expect in Paris Hotels

Most of the places I recommend are small, family-run hotels. The owners are usually involved, often speak English, and take pride in their service. You'll find rooms that are clean, quiet, and cozy—maybe a little snug—but full of charm.

A double room in this type of hotel generally runs **€130–200 per night**, with a private bathroom included. If you're on a tighter budget, you can find something more basic (sometimes with a shared toilet/shower) for around **€70–100**. On the higher end, boutique or luxury hotels with larger rooms and more services can easily reach **€300–400** or more.

Rooms with twin beds or bathtubs often cost a little more than those with just a double bed and shower. Elevators are common but often tiny. Older buildings may have none at all, so check if that's important to you—especially if you're carrying luggage or have mobility concerns.

Hotel Breakfasts

Most hotels offer breakfast, though it's rarely included in the room rate. Expect to pay **€10–20** for a self-service buffet with the usual: croissants, baguettes, jam, butter, cheese, yogurt, cereal, juice, and coffee. It's convenient, but if you prefer to eat like a Parisian, just step outside and grab a pastry and espresso at the corner bakery for a fraction of the price.

Understanding the Star Ratings

France uses an official star system (from 0 to 5), but don't read too much into it. It reflects amenities more than atmosphere. A one-star hotel can still be charming and spotless, and a four-star might just have bigger rooms and a nicer elevator. Focus more on location, comfort, and reviews than the star count.

Making a Reservation

Once you've settled on your travel dates, book early—especially for spring, summer, or holiday seasons.

The best way to book is through a hotel's **official website** or **by contacting them directly** by email or phone. Avoid third-party booking sites if you want to keep things flexible or make special requests. When you contact a hotel, be ready with:

- Room type and number of guests
- Dates (in **day/month/year** format)
- Twin or double bed preference
- Budget range
- Arrival time (especially if it's after 17:00)
- Any extras (balcony, bathtub, quiet room, etc.)

- Mention any promo codes or special offers

Hotels usually ask for a **credit card** to hold your room. If their site doesn't have a secure form, give your details by phone instead of email.

If your plans change, cancel as early as possible—many places have strict cancellation policies. It's also smart to **reconfirm your stay** a few days before arrival, especially for small hotels or guesthouses (*chambres d'hôtes*).

When booking a place to stay in Paris, your budget is a key factor. Use this pricing guide to get a sense of what to expect based on your travel style.

Hotel Price Categories (High Season, Double Room, No Breakfast)

- **$$$$ Splurge** – Over €300: Expect luxury: spacious rooms, designer furnishings, professional staff, and top-tier locations. Often includes a spa, concierge, and full-service amenities.

- **$$$ Pricier** – €200–300: Boutique hotels, stylish decor, historic buildings, or locations just steps from major landmarks. These rooms usually offer more space and comfort.

- **$$ Moderate** – €130–200: Clean, centrally located, comfortable hotels. These are solid picks for most travelers. Many are small, family-run places or local chains.

- **$ Budget** – €70–130: Basic rooms in older buildings or quieter neighborhoods. Some may lack elevators or modern bathrooms, but they're generally safe and functional.

- **¢ Backpacker** – Under €70: Hostels, shared facilities, or very simple hotel rooms. You'll need to compromise on space, privacy, or location, but it's possible to find deals.

What Star Ratings Mean in France

The French hotel rating system runs from **zero to five stars**, based on official criteria like room size, amenities, reception hours, and whether there's an elevator. It doesn't always reflect charm or cleanliness.

Even a **one- or two-star** hotel can be cozy and welcoming. A **three-star** generally means reliable comfort, while **four- and five-star** places add service and extras (but not always character).

Unless otherwise noted:

- **Credit cards** are accepted

- **Wi-Fi** is free

- **Some staff speak English**

Budget Tips for Sleeping in Paris

Compare Rates

Always check the **hotel's official website** in addition to big booking platforms like Booking.com or Expedia. Some hotels offer cash discounts or lower prices if you contact them directly.

Consider Location

Staying a few blocks away from the Seine or major attractions can lower prices significantly. Just make sure you're close to a Métro stop—ideally on a major line like 1, 4, or RER B.

Look Into Apartments

For longer stays or small groups, an apartment can save you money, especially if you want a kitchen or laundry.

Options include:

- https://www.airbnb.com/

- https://www.booking.com/

- https://www.vrbo.com/

- https://www.flipkey.com/

French apartments tend to be small, and many don't have elevators, air conditioning, or dryers. Still, they offer privacy, a local feel, and a chance to shop at Paris markets and cook like a local.

Stay a Bit Longer

Some hotels and apartments offer discounts for stays of 3+ nights. Always ask when booking directly.

Travel Off-Season

From November through March (except holidays), you'll often find the best rates, more availability, and quieter hotels.

Want help matching a neighborhood to your price range or travel style? I can suggest sample hotels, too—just say the word.

Near Marais

The Marais is stylish, central, and full of character. Think old stone buildings, hidden courtyards, and lively cafés. You're walking distance to the Seine, Place des Vosges, and Pompidou. Closest métro stops: Saint-Paul, Hôtel de Ville, and Chemin Vert.

€€€ Expensive: €200–300

Hôtel Bourg Tibourg

Elegant, intimate, and very Parisian. Small, dimly lit rooms with rich fabrics and a moody boutique vibe. Some rooms face the quiet inner courtyard. Just off Rue Vieille du Temple, a perfect location. 19 Rue du Bourg Tibourg, +33 1 42 78 47 39.

Le Pavillon de la Reine & Spa**

A hidden oasis tucked into Place des Vosges. Luxurious rooms, a peaceful private garden, and a full spa. It's quiet and upscale, ideal if you want to splurge without flashy luxury. 28 Place des Vosges, +33 1 40 29 19 19.

Hôtel du Petit Moulin**

Designed by Christian Lacroix, this small hotel is full of quirky charm. Each room is different—colorful, artistic, and playful. Good for travelers looking for a creative, offbeat stay. 29-31 Rue de Poitou, +33 1 42 74 10 10.

Hôtel Les Bains Paris***

A high-end, design-focused hotel with history—it used to be a famous nightclub. Polished, modern rooms and a sleek restaurant/bar. Trendy crowd. Located near Arts et Métiers. 7 Rue du Bourg l'Abbé, +33 1 42 77 07 07.

€€ Moderate: €130–200

Hotel Turenne Le Marais*

A solid pick if you want comfort and convenience without paying top prices. Clean, well-kept rooms with A/C and updated bathrooms. Steps from Saint-Paul métro. 6 Rue de Turenne, +33 1 42 78 43 25.

Hôtel Le Compostelle*

No-frills but central and functional. Rooms are straightforward with a classic feel. Some are small, but it's quiet at night, and the staff is helpful. 31 Rue du Roi de Sicile, +33 1 42 72 76 17.

Hotel Georgette*

A colorful, modern hotel tucked near the Pompidou. Rooms are compact but well-designed, with playful touches. It's artsy, bright, and good for solo travelers or couples. 36 Rue du Grenier Saint-Lazare, +33 1 44 61 10 10.

Hotel Jeanne d'Arc Le Marais*

Cozy and casual with a friendly staff. Nicely decorated rooms in a calm corner near Place Sainte-Catherine. The rooms are small but charming. 3 Rue de Jarente, +33 1 48 87 62 11.

€ Budget: €70–130

Hôtel Rivoli*

An older hotel with basic, clean rooms in a top location—directly on Rue de Rivoli. It's simple and great for budget travelers who just need a clean bed and a private bathroom. 44 Rue de Rivoli, +33 1 48 87 41 22.

Hôtel Paris France

A good budget find with a bit of character. Rooms are plain but spacious for the price, and the location near République is convenient. Ask for a room facing the quiet back side. 72 Rue de Turbigo, +33 1 42 72 14 16.

¢ Backpacker: Under €70

The People Paris Marais

Modern hostel setup with a great location near Canal Saint-Martin (10 min.. walk from the Marais edge). Clean dorms, private rooms, a lively rooftop bar, and good common areas. 17 Boulevard Morland, +33 1 86 65 39 73.

Auberge de Jeunesse MIJE Marais

Three historic buildings—Fourcy, Fauconnier, and Maubuisson—all offer basic but well-located hostel stays. Simple rooms with bunk beds and shared facilities. No-frills, safe, and unbeatable location for the price. Book through the MIJE site. Headquarters: 6 Rue de Fourcy, +33 1 42 74 23 45.

Where to Stay Near Luxembourg Garden

This neighborhood has that classic Left Bank vibe—bookstores, cafés, quiet courtyards, and a famous park right nearby. It's a great base for exploring both central and southern Paris. Nearby Métro stations include Cluny-La Sorbonne, St. Sulpice, Mabillon, and Odéon.

$$$$ Splurge: Over €300

Hôtel Esprit Saint Germain**

This five-star boutique hotel offers discreet luxury in a quiet spot just off Boulevard Saint-Germain. The décor is stylish yet homey, with fireplaces in the lounges and a cozy library for guests. Some rooms overlook rooftops, and there's a wellness room with a sauna and fitness gear.

22 Rue Saint-Sulpice, +33 1 53 10 55 55.

Relais Christine**

A hidden gem just north of the park, this former abbey has been turned into a romantic retreat with elegant rooms and a lush private garden. The vaulted spa is one of the prettiest in Paris.

3 Rue Christine, +33 1 40 51 60 80.

$$$ Expensive: €200–300

Hôtel Le Senat**

Just steps from the Luxembourg Gardens, this sleek boutique hotel has modern rooms with deep tones, some offering balconics or park views. A quiet and stylish base near the Sorbonne.

10 Rue de Vaugirard, +33 1 43 54 54 54.

Hôtel Villa d'Estrées**

Well-located near Odéon, this small hotel has warm colors, large rooms, and a relaxed, intimate feel. Ideal for travelers who want a central base that still feels like a retreat.

17 Rue Gît-le-Cœur, +33 1 55 42 71 11.

Hôtel Le Clos Medicis*

Across from the Luxembourg Garden, this 38-room hotel combines classic wood-beam charm with subtle luxury. A small garden terrace offers a rare peaceful corner.

56 Rue Monsieur le Prince, +33 1 43 29 10 20.

Hôtel La Perle*

Simple, clean, and stylish, with exposed beams and a pleasant breakfast room facing a little patio. The rooms are compact but quiet and well-kept.

14 Rue des Canettes, +33 1 43 29 10 10.

$$ Moderate: €130–200

Hôtel André Latin*

This stylish retro-chic hotel near the Panthéon features clean, updated rooms with a mid-century twist. It's good value for the location, and the vibe is relaxed. 50 Rue Gay-Lussac, +33 1 40 46 08 88.**

Hôtel des 3 Collèges

No-frills but dependable, right across from the Sorbonne. Rooms are basic but clean, with decent space and solid value for the area. 16 Rue Cujas, +33 1 46 34 10 12.

Hôtel Clément*

Right near Marché St. Germain and Rue de Buci, this 28-room hotel is great for foodies and shoppers. The rooms are small but efficient, and the location is hard to beat. 6 Rue Clément, +33 1 43 26 53 60.

$ Budget: €70–130

Hôtel du Brésil

A no-frills option tucked behind the Panthéon. Rooms are basic, a bit dated, but clean and budget-friendly. Friendly staff, decent breakfast, and excellent location. 10 Rue Le Goff, +33 1 43 54 76 60.

Hôtel Stella

One of the most old-school cheap stays in the city—bare-bones, no elevator, and cash-only—but it has loyal fans for its quirky charm and unbeatable price. Shared bathrooms. 62 Rue Monsieur le Prince, +33 1 43 26 96 27.

The Rue Cler neighborhood is one of Paris' most pleasant and practical areas to stay. Just a short walk from the Eiffel Tower, this area feels lively yet safe, residential but still central. You're close to markets, bakeries, cafés, and three useful Métro stops: **École Militaire**, **La Tour-Maubourg**, and **Invalides**. It's ideal for first-time visitors, families, or anyone who prefers a calm base with charm and convenience.

High-End (Over €300)

Le Cinq Codet – 4

A sleek, modern hotel tucked behind the Invalides. Rooms are minimalist and spacious, some with Eiffel Tower views. The on-site spa and courtyard terrace make it a serene spot after a day of walking.

5 Rue Louis Codet | +33 1 53 85 15 60

Hotel Thoumieux – 4

Above a top-tier restaurant, this boutique hotel has only a few rooms, each with bold, artistic decor. Feels like a stylish Parisian home with personal touches and standout service.

79 Rue Saint-Dominique | +33 1 47 05 49 75

Mid-Range (€200–300)

Hotel Juliana Paris – 5★

Elegant and discreet, with plush rooms and old-world flair. There's a rooftop terrace and a small gym. Quiet location near the Seine, great for evening strolls.

10-12 Rue Cognacq-Jay | +33 1 47 05 79 79

Hotel La Comtesse – 4★

A stylish boutique stay with Eiffel Tower views from many rooms. Think clean lines, velvet accents, and a great café downstairs. Good value for the view.

29 Avenue de Tourville | +33 1 45 51 29 29

Hotel Le Walt – 4★

Classic meets modern here, with rooms decorated like mini galleries. Right near Rue Cler and metro access, but tucked just far enough for peace.

37 Avenue de la Motte-Picquet | +33 1 45 51 55 83

Moderate (€130–200)

Hotel Eiffel Rive Gauche – 3★

Simple, no-frills hotel with small rooms and helpful staff. Quiet location on a side street, with some rooms offering Eiffel glimpses.

6 Rue du Gros Caillou | +33 1 47 05 25 15

Hotel Amélie – 3★

Charming, colorful, and relaxed. Rooms are compact but cheerful. Just around the corner from Rue Cler's cafés and market stalls.

5 Rue Amélie | +33 1 45 51 74 30

Hotel de l'Alma Paris – 3★

Budget-friendly, clean, and extremely central. Rooms are straightforward, and the location puts you in the middle of everything.

32 Rue de l'Exposition | +33 1 45 51 55 83

Budget (€70–130)

Hotel Derby Eiffel – 3★

Older, traditional hotel with Eiffel Tower views from some rooms. Reliable, with decent-sized rooms and a good location near Rue Cler and the Champs de Mars.

5 Avenue Duquesne | +33 1 47 05 12 05

Hotel Royal Phare – 2★

Basic and affordable, with compact rooms and unbeatable metro access. Nothing fancy but great for travelers who prioritize location.

40 Avenue de la Motte-Picquet | +33 1 47 05 25 81

Near Montmartre

Montmartre feels like a village perched on a hill, full of artists, cafés, steep stairways, and scenic views. Staying here gives you a more local, laid-back Paris experience. It's ideal for those who don't mind a few climbs and want charm over centrality. Closest Metro stations: **Abbesses**, **Anvers**, **Lamarck–Caulaincourt**.

$$$$ Splurge: Over €300

Maison Souquet***

A hidden five-star gem just steps from Pigalle. The atmosphere is romantic and plush, with velvet-lined rooms, a secret bar, and a private spa. Elegant and theatrical.

10 Rue de Bruxelles, +33 1 48 78 55 55

Manolita Paris***

An intimate boutique hotel with only ten high-design rooms. Everything feels custom-made and private. Located right off busy Rue Lepic but well insulated from noise.

1 Rue Lepic, +33 1 87 44 15 15

$$$ Expensive: €200–300

Hôtel Particulier Montmartre**

A stylish mansion with only a few large suites, set between two hidden alleys. You're surrounded by greenery, and there's a courtyard restaurant open to locals, too.

23 Avenue Junot, +33 1 53 41 81 40

Hôtel Monsieur Aristide

Modern, creative decor with a bohemian vibe. It's peaceful, close to Sacré-Cœur, and has a lovely courtyard café. A good mix of class and comfort.

3 Rue Aristide Bruant, +33 1 87 44 64 24

Hôtel Le Relais Montmartre**

Traditional charm with exposed beams and vintage decor. Located on a quiet side street just off the bustle of Rue Lepic. Solid choice for couples.

6 Rue Constance, +33 1 42 64 41 00

$$ Moderate: €130–200

Hôtel des Arts Montmartre*

Friendly and consistently praised. Rooms are simple, some have great rooftop views. Walkable to shops, bakeries, and Sacré-Cœur.

5 Rue Tholozé, +33 1 46 06 30 52

Timhotel Montmartre*

Rooms are basic but clean, with some of the best balcony views in the area. Located right by Place Émile-Goudeau and a few minutes from Abbesses.

11 Rue Ravignan, +33 1 46 06 18 38

Hôtel Basss*

Trendy, compact, and well-located for budget-conscious travelers who want a modern look. Steps from cafés and nightlife.

57 Rue des Abbesses, +33 1 42 51 50 00

$ Budget: €70–130

Hotel Luxelthe

Simple and functional. Recent renovations make this a decent pick for the price. Right between the energy of Pigalle and the charm of Montmartre.

13 Rue Houdon, +33 1 42 54 43 56

Hotel Montpellier

An older hotel, very basic and worn, but very cheap. You'll be close to Sacré-Cœur and the Metro. Great for backpackers on a tight budget.

64 Boulevard de Rochechouart, +33 1 48 78 45 26

FOOD AND RESTAURANTS

The Paris food scene is always buzzing. It's inspired entire books, careers, and obsessions. In this city, meals aren't rushed—they're part of the culture. You'll see Parisians spending hours at cafés with a drink, some bread, and conversation. Whether you're splurging on a three-course dinner or grabbing a baguette to go, tasting Paris is part of experiencing it.

You don't need to spend a lot to enjoy great food here. Even if you're staying in a budget hotel, make space in your budget—and your schedule—for at least one proper Parisian meal. I've listed a range of places, from quick, affordable eats to elegant restaurants worth dressing up for. Many are located near top sights or hotels I've recommended, so it's easy to plan meals around your sightseeing.

How Locals Eat

Follow the French daily rhythm. A typical day might start with coffee and a croissant at the counter of a corner café. Lunch runs from about 12:00 to 14:30 and can be a hot dish, a good salad, or a sandwich enjoyed in a park. Late afternoon is café time again—a glass of wine or a coffee with friends. Dinner usually starts after 19:30 and is when meals become slower, longer, and more social.

How Restaurants Work

Most restaurants open for dinner around 19:00 or 19:30 and fill up quickly between 20:00 and 21:00. Many close on Sundays or Mondays. Cafés and brasseries stay open longer and offer more flexibility, but dinner still tends to follow a relaxed pace.

A full dinner might include an apéritif, a starter (entrée), main dish (plat), cheese, dessert, coffee, and maybe even a digestif. But don't worry—you don't have to eat it all. Many locals just order two courses, like a starter and a main or a main and a dessert.

Menus often include a fixed-price "formula" with two or three courses. It's usually a good value, even at nicer restaurants. Some dishes come with a surcharge (marked as "supplément" or "sup."). Tap water is free if you ask for it: "Une carafe d'eau, s'il vous plaît." Bread is always complimentary.

Tips and Etiquette

The bill almost always includes tax and service, so tipping is optional. If the service is great, you can leave a euro or two on the table—but it's not expected. Waiters don't hover, and they won't bring the bill unless you ask. Say "L'addition, s'il vous plaît" when you're ready.

Also, don't wave or snap—get your server's attention by meeting their eyes and politely raising your hand. At cafés, outdoor tables may allow smoking, while indoor seating is non-smoking by law.

Paris Dining Etiquette

In this guide, prices are shown with dollar symbols to give a rough idea of what you'll pay for a typical main course.

A single dollar sign ($) means budget places– like crêpe stands, sandwich shops, and basic takeout—where you can eat for under €20.

Double dollar signs ($$) refer to moderately priced spots, such as cafés, bistros, and brasseries, where most mains fall between €20 and €30.

Triple dollar signs ($$$) are for pricier restaurants, with mains around €30 to €40.

Quadruple dollar signs ($$$$) point to high-end dining experiences where a main course costs over €40.

In France, take your time at the table. Dining is meant to be slow and social. Waiters won't rush you, and they won't bring the check unless you ask—just say, *"L'addition, s'il vous plaît."* Enjoy the pacing, chat with your server, appreciate the presentation, and make the meal part of your day—not just a pause in it.

Bon appétit.

Cafés and Brasseries

These are casual, welcoming spots where you can sit down anytime of day for a meal, a snack, or just a drink. Less formal than traditional restaurants, cafés and brasseries stay open between regular meal times, which means you can eat a salad, sandwich, or hot dish even in the late afternoon or evening.

You're free to order whatever suits your mood—a *plat du jour* (daily special), main course, hearty salad, croque monsieur (grilled ham and cheese), omelet, soup, or dessert. While it's uncommon to share main dishes in France, it's fine to split a starter or dessert.

Most places have outdoor seating—great for people-watching—with awnings or heaters to keep things cozy in cooler months. Crêperies are also a nice, casual alternative. They serve savory galettes (made with buckwheat flour) and sweet dessert crêpes. They're quick, tasty, and usually cheap.

Note that prices can change depending on where you sit. Drinks and even food cost more at a table than they do at the bar (called *le comptoir*). If you're just grabbing a coffee or a glass of wine and don't mind standing or sitting at the counter, it's a way to save a couple of euros.

Picnicking

Picnicking in Paris is easy—and often delicious. You'll find takeout food all over the city, especially at *charcuteries* (deli-style butcher shops), *traiteurs* (takeout shops), and bakeries. They'll have things like pâté, quiche, small pizzas, cold salads, rotisserie chicken, or hot dishes packed into little trays (*barquettes*) that you can carry away with a fork (*fourchette*). You can even ask to have things reheated (*chauffé*), and they'll often wrap it all up neatly for you.

A typical picnic might include a warm dish or some cold cuts from a deli, a crusty baguette from a *boulangerie*, a soft cheese or two from a *fromagerie*, and some fruit or wine from a local market. You can also pick up drinks and extras at a regular supermarket (*supermarché*), though the quality isn't as special.

Try things you wouldn't normally—some funky-smelling cheese, a pâté you've never heard of, or a tiny glass jar of yogurt. Paris makes it easy to be adventurous.

Some great spots to enjoy a picnic in central Paris: the garden at Palais Royal, Place des Vosges, the tip of Île de la Cité near Notre-Dame, and the Tuileries Garden near the Louvre. Grab a bench or find a shady patch of grass and enjoy the simple pleasure of eating well outside.

French Cuisine

One of the great joys of being in Paris is that you can taste the flavors of all of France without ever leaving the city. While many Paris restaurants serve a mix of traditional French dishes, others specialize in food from specific regions.

From Burgundy, you'll find coq au vin (chicken simmered in red wine), bœuf bourguignon (beef stew), and escargots (snails in garlic butter). Normandy and Brittany bring seafood like mussels and oysters, along with crepes and cider. Dishes *à la provençale*—from Provence—tend to include tomatoes, olive oil, garlic, and herbs. The south's Côte d'Azur is famous for *bouillabaisse* (a rich fish stew), while the southwest offers *foie gras* and *confit de canard* (slow-cooked duck). In the northeast, Alsace contributes *choucroute garnie*—a mountain of sauerkraut with sausage and ham.

Food

Parisians love steak in all its forms, including *steak frites* (steak and fries) and *steak tartare* (raw, finely chopped steak with egg and seasoning). Other popular picks include *poulet rôti* (roast chicken), *gigot d'agneau* (roast leg of lamb), *saumon* (salmon), and at Christmas, fresh *huîtres* (raw oysters from Brittany).

French sauces are an art form. The five "mother sauces" include *béchamel* (creamy white sauce), *espagnole* (dark brown, stock-based), *velouté* (lighter and made with stock), *tomate*, and *hollandaise* (egg yolks and butter). These form the base for dozens of others.

Cheese is a serious business. From *Brie de Meaux* (mild and creamy) and *Camembert* (stronger and soft) to *chèvre* (goat cheese) and *Roquefort* (a blue cheese from the south), there's something for every taste. Many restaurants offer a *plateau de fromages*—a cheese plate—either instead of or along with dessert.

Speaking of dessert, a *café gourmand* is a great choice: a small espresso served with a few mini desserts selected by the chef. Other classic sweets include *crème brûlée*, *tarte Tatin* (upside-down caramelized apple tart), and *mousse au chocolat*.

Wine and Apéritifs in France

In France, no meal feels truly complete without a glass of wine. Even a basic *vin du pays*—local table wine—can beautifully complement your dish. Most restaurants offer house wines either by the glass or in a small *pichet* (carafe). For reds, consider a bottle from Côtes du Rhône or Languedoc; for whites, Burgundy and Alsace are excellent choices. When the weather heats up, a crisp, chilled rosé is a refreshing option. Want to indulge a little? A rich Bordeaux or a refined Pinot Noir from Burgundy won't disappoint.

Before dinner, many locals skip wine altogether and go for an *apéritif*, a pre-meal drink to open the appetite. Common choices include Champagne, a cold beer, or classic French favorites like Kir (white wine with blackcurrant liqueur) or Pastis, the anise-scented spirit from Provence. Some of the country's finest beers come from the Alsace region—look for names like Kronenbourg 1664 or the fuller-bodied Pelforth. On a warm day, cool off with a *panaché*, a light mix of beer and lemon soda that's perfect for sipping in the sun.

Caffeteries

Coffee habits are specific here. After a meal, Parisians often order *un café* (a small espresso), *une noisette* (an espresso with a touch of milk), or *café crème* (espresso with steamed milk, similar to a latte). If you're looking for something non-alcoholic and uniquely French, try a *diabolo menthe*—mint syrup with lemon soda. And if you order a Coke, don't expect ice unless you ask—Parisians rarely use it.

Around Marais area

This stylish district offers a blend of historic charm and trendy energy. Perfect for strolling, shopping, and eating well. Ideal for both casual bites and long, social dinners. Good for lunch in the sun or dinner before a night out. Metro stops: St-Paul, Hôtel de Ville, Chemin Vert, and Bastille.

$$$ Robert et Louise

An old-school favorite with communal tables, wood-fired meats, and serious rustic vibes. Order the côte de boeuf for two and a bottle of red. Open daily for dinner, lunch on weekends. 64 Rue Vieille du Temple, +33 1 42 78 55 89.

$$$ Les Philosophes

Bustling, classic Marais café with tightly packed tables, a solid bistro menu, and great people-watching. Their onion soup and duck confit are house favorites. 28 Rue Vieille du Temple, +33 1 48 87 49 64.

$$$ L'Ange 20

Tiny bistro near the Picasso Museum with modern French cooking, friendly staff, and great value for the quality. Reserve ahead, as seating is limited. Closed Sunday and Monday. 44 Rue des Tournelles, +33 1 49 96 58 39.

$$ Breizh Café

Trendy crêperie with Breton specialties: buckwheat galettes, cider, and excellent salted butter caramel crêpes. Expect a wait or book ahead. Multiple locations; this one's at 109 Rue Vieille du Temple, +33 1 42 72 13 77.

$$ Miznon

Israeli street food in a loud, casual space—get the lamb kebab or roasted cauliflower. Great for a fast, flavor-packed lunch. No reservations. 22 Rue des Ecouffes, +33 1 42 74 83 58.

$ Les Petites Bouchées

Affordable, modern French food with small plates and natural wines. Cozy and relaxed, it's good for a casual dinner. Closed Mon–Tue. 4 Rue de Jouy, +33 6 64 13 08 45.

$ La Droguerie

Tiny crêpe stand near Rue des Rosiers serving cheap, tasty sweet and savory crêpes to go. Ideal for a quick snack. 56 Rue des Rosiers.

$ L'As du Fallafel

Paris' most famous falafel spot. Always crowded, always fast. Go for the "fallafel spécial." Closed Saturdays. 34 Rue des Rosiers, +33 1 48 87 63 60.

Around Ile St. Louis area

Quiet, romantic, and a bit off the tourist path, this island is ideal for a relaxed evening. Expect charm, narrow cobbled streets, and small, candlelit restaurants. Metro stop: Pont Marie.

$$$ Mon Vieil Ami

A modern bistro in a traditional setting, this spot features communal tables and refined, veggie-forward French cuisine with quality meats and fish. Quiet, candlelit, and intimate. Closed Monday and Tuesday. 69 Rue Saint-Louis en l'Île, +33 1 40 46 01 35.

$$$ Sorza

Small, elegant restaurant that blends Italian flair with French technique. Try the burrata or truffle risotto. Friendly service and is perfect for a romantic dinner. Closed Wednesday. 51 Rue Saint-Louis en l'Île, +33 1 43 54 16 88.

$$ Brasserie de l'Isle Saint-Louis

Old-school charm with a terrace right along the Seine. A great place for classic Alsatian fare like choucroute and duck confit. It gets busy—go early for a river view. Open daily. 55 Quai de Bourbon, +33 1 43 54 02 59.

$$ Le Saint Régis

Stylish corner café with a classic Parisian brasserie vibe, serving reliable café staples like croque monsieur, beef tartare, and steak-frites. Nice for breakfast, lunch, or dinner. 6 Rue Jean du Bellay, +33 1 43 54 59 41.

$$ La Brasserie de l'Île

Simple, no-fuss French food in a prime location, perfect for an easy lunch after a walk around the island. Try the duck confit or onion soup. Outdoor seating is a plus. 51 Rue Saint-Louis en l'Île, +33 1 43 26 64 94.

$$ Le Flore en l'Île

A bright and friendly café that's open all day, ideal for a crêpe, salad, or even just coffee with a view of Notre-Dame. Also good for a quiet breakfast. 42 Quai d'Orléans, +33 1 43 25 76 67.

$ Crêperie Saint-Louis

Tiny, casual spot offering simple and tasty Breton crêpes, both savory (galettes) and sweet. Very affordable, very popular with locals. 9 Rue Saint-Louis en l'Île, +33 1 43 54 75 73.

$ Berthillon Glacier

Paris' most famous ice cream is sold at dozens of cafés on the island, but head to the original counter for the full experience. Closed Monday and Tuesday. 29-31 Rue Saint-Louis en l'Île.

Around Rue Cler

Whether you're in the mood for a refined culinary experience or a simple café meal, this neighborhood offers plenty of options. Here are fresh picks locals love and visitors return to.

$$$$ L'Ami Jean

Inventive Basque-influenced fine dining in a cozy, lively setting. The chef is known for bold flavors and an ever-changing tasting menu. A splurge worth every bite. Reservations essential.

27 Rue Malar, Tel. +33 1 47 05 86 89

$$$ Les Cocottes – Christian Constant

Modern, elegant, and unfussy. Dishes are served in cast-iron cocottes with French classics reimagined in creative ways. No reservations—arrive early.

135 Rue Saint-Dominique, Tel. +33 1 45 50 10 31

$$$ Restaurant Sylvestre Wahid

Two Michelin stars with a sleek, contemporary vibe. Refined plates combining seasonal French ingredients with international inspiration. Tasting menus only.

79 Rue Saint-Dominique, Tel. +33 1 47 05 79 00

$$$ Chez Pippo

Italian charm just steps from the Eiffel Tower. Known for hearty pastas, wood-fired pizzas, and an energetic atmosphere. Reserve for dinner.

31 Avenue de la Bourdonnais, Tel. +33 1 47 05 95 94

$$ La Veraison

Friendly and flavorful. Seasonal cuisine with a modern touch, strong wine list, and fair prices. A neighborhood favorite that feels like a hidden gem. Closed Sundays.

64 Rue de la Croix Nivert, Tel. +33 1 45 32 39 29

$$ Le Florimond

Charming and consistently praised for warm hospitality and quality French dishes. Duck confit and seasonal plates stand out. Closed Sundays and Mondays.

19 Avenue de la Motte-Picquet, Tel. +33 1 45 55 40 38

$$ Bistro Saint-Dominique

Bright and relaxed with an elegant touch. Great for lunch or a quiet dinner. Serves elevated bistro fare in a stylish interior or on the terrace. Open daily.

131 Rue Saint-Dominique, Tel. +33 1 47 53 73 34

$$ L'Abreuvoir

Solid choice for classic French comfort food with a local twist. Duck breast, beef tartare, and daily specials deliver satisfying flavors. Closed Sundays.

28 Rue de l'Exposition, Tel. +33 1 45 51 30 28

$$ Café Constant

Welcoming bistro with honest cooking and no pretense. Think roasted chicken, fish of the day, and rich desserts. Walk-ins only.

139 Rue Saint-Dominique, Tel. +33 1 47 53 73 34

$ Le Petit Riche

Classic French eatery with an old-school vibe and surprisingly reasonable prices. Hearty portions and friendly service. Open daily.

25 Rue Le Peletier, Tel. +33 1 47 70 68 68

$ Le Petit Tonneau

Rustic and cheerful, this small bistro serves regional French dishes at great prices. Don't miss the cassoulet. Closed Mondays.

20 Rue Surcouf, Tel. +33 1 47 05 09 01

$ Breizh Café

Trendy Breton crêperie with organic buckwheat galettes and imaginative fillings. Top-notch cider too. Book ahead or expect a wait.

1 Rue de l'Odéon, Tel. +33 1 42 49 34 73

BEST VIEWS OF PARIS

Paris is beautiful at any angle, but some spots really stand out when you want to take in the full sweep of the city. Whether you're looking for iconic landmarks, romantic sunset spots, or just a quiet place to soak in the skyline, these viewpoints are worth the climb or ride.

Eiffel Tower (Tour Eiffel)

Of course, the Eiffel Tower tops the list. From its upper deck, you'll see all of Paris laid out before you—the Seine snaking through the city, the golden dome of Les Invalides, and the wide boulevards stretching toward the horizon. It's busiest around sunset, so book your timed ticket in advance.

Arc de Triomphe

From the top of this famous monument, you get a striking aerial view straight down the Champs-Élysées. Look out for the twelve avenues radiating like a star from the roundabout—this is the city's geometric heart. The climb is a bit steep (284 steps), but the reward is panoramic.

Sacré-Cœur in Montmartre

Perched on the highest hill in Paris, the steps in front of Sacré-Cœur Basilica offer a sweeping view of rooftops and spires. Come early in the morning or in the evening when the city lights begin to sparkle. The dome of the basilica itself offers an even higher lookout (ticket required).

Montparnasse Tower

Though it's not the prettiest building in town, the 56th-floor observation deck has a major advantage: It's the only view that includes the Eiffel Tower itself. Come for sunset and watch the city shift into night. It's less crowded than the Eiffel Tower and much quicker to get up.

Galeries Lafayette Rooftop

Right in the heart of the shopping district, the rooftop terrace of Galeries Lafayette (free and open during store hours) gives you a great view of the Opéra Garnier with the Eiffel Tower in the distance. Stop by for a photo or even a snack from the rooftop café.

Place du Trocadéro

On the opposite side of the Seine from the Eiffel Tower, this plaza offers a perfect ground-level view of the tower. It's popular with photographers at sunrise and night, especially when the lights and sparkle show come on.

Centre Pompidou Rooftop

While visiting the modern art museum, don't skip the rooftop terrace. It offers unexpected views over central Paris, with Notre-Dame, Sacré-Cœur, and the Eiffel Tower all visible in the distance. There's also a café where you can sit and enjoy the view with a drink.

Printemps and BHV Marais Rooftops

Both department stores have terraces with surprisingly good views—Printemps overlooks the Opéra district, and BHV looks out over the Marais and Hotel de Ville. A good place for a coffee break with a view.

Pont Alexandre III and Pont Neuf

If you're looking for a scenic walk, stop mid-bridge on these two. Pont Alexandre III has dramatic views of the Eiffel Tower and Invalides, while Pont Neuf (the city's oldest bridge) offers peaceful river views, especially around sunset.

Parc de Belleville and Parc des Buttes-Chaumont

These less-visited parks in the northeast offer more local atmospheres and unique skyline views. Belleville gives you a wide stretch of eastern Paris; Buttes-Chaumont has charming hills, a suspension bridge, and a little temple with a view over Montmartre.

SAFETY AND EMERGENCIES

Health and Safety Assistance

For any emergency—ambulance, police, or fire—call **112** from any phone. It's the universal European emergency number and works from mobile or landlines.

If you feel unwell or need quick medical advice, go to a **pharmacy** first. French pharmacists are trained to give basic consultations and can recommend over-the-counter medication or refer you to a doctor. Hotel staff can also help connect you with local medical services.

English-Speaking Medical Services in Paris

If you require medical care during your stay, the following facilities provide assistance in English and are trusted by both locals and international visitors.

American Hospital of Paris

A private, internationally recognized hospital offering full medical services, including emergency care, with English-speaking staff across all departments.

Address: 63 Boulevard Victor Hugo, Neuilly-sur-Seine

Open: 24/7

Phone: +33 1 46 41 25 25

Website: www.american-hospital.org

Pharmacie des Champs

Located on the Champs-Élysées, this pharmacy has English-speaking staff and provides a wide selection of medications and over-the-counter treatments.

Address: 84 Avenue des Champs-Élysées, 75008 Paris

Phone: +33 1 45 62 02 41

Pharmacie Européenne

Open 24 hours, this well-stocked pharmacy near Place de Clichy offers multilingual service, including

English, and is a reliable option for travelers.

Address: 6 Place de Clichy, 75009 Paris

Phone: +33 1 48 74 65 18

Telemedicine - Doctors in France

This service connects you with English-speaking doctors for video consultations or in-person appointments. Fast, reliable, and designed with travelers in mind.

Website: www.doctorsinfrance.com

Theft or Loss

Paris is generally safe, but **petty theft is a real issue**, especially in crowded places like the Metro, tourist hotspots, and train stations. Most incidents involve pickpocketing or phone snatching.
Here are a few simple precautions:

- Keep your **phone out of sight** in public transport.
- Use a **money belt** or under-clothing pouch for valuables.
- If carrying a bag, wear it **crossbody** and keep it in front of you.
- **Don't leave bags hanging on chairs** at cafés or resting at your feet.
- If your **passport** is lost or stolen, contact the **U.S. Embassy**: 2 Avenue Gabriel, near Place de la Concorde, Mo: Champs-Élysées Clemenceau. Tel: +33 1 43 12 22 22.

If your **credit card** is lost or stolen, call the 24-hour U.S. numbers to cancel immediately:

- **Visa:** +1-303-967-1096
- **MasterCard:** +1-636-722-7111
- **American Express:** +1-336-393-1111

For **lost items,** contact the Paris Lost & Found Office (**Bureau des Objets Trouvés**) at 36 Rue des Morillons, Mo: Convention. Open Mon–Fri, 8:30–17:00. Tel: +33 1 53 71 53 71.

Street Smarts

Pedestrian safety isn't always a given in Paris. Cars, buses, and especially **bikes and scooters** may not yield, even at crosswalks.

- Always **look both ways,** even on one-way streets—bikes often go against traffic.

- **Don't trust the green light completely.** Watch the road before crossing.

- **Sidewalks sometimes double as bike lanes**—stay alert for cyclists.

- Late at night, stay on **well-lit, busy streets**, especially around the outer arrondissements.

CONCLUSION

Thanks so much for walking through Paris with me.

This guide was written with a lot of love—for the city itself, and for the joy of helping others discover it. Paris has a way of pulling you in with its beauty, its energy, and its deep history. I hope this book made your time here a little easier, a little richer, and maybe even a little more magical.

There's always more to see in Paris. The famous sights are just the beginning. The real wonder is in the little surprises: turning a corner and finding a quiet square, stumbling into a bookstore you weren't looking for, or sitting by the river as the city lights start to glow. Those are the moments that stick with you.

So don't rush. Let yourself wander. Slow down, take it all in, and let Paris happen around you. That's how the best memories are made.

I hope this guide gave you the confidence to explore freely and enjoy it all—big and small.

Thanks again for bringing this book along. I'm wishing you a beautiful stay in the City of Light, and a trip full of stories you'll never forget.

Bon voyage,

Adrian Nakamura

Printed in Dunstable, United Kingdom

65421344R00105